# How to Teach Writing Across the Curriculum: Ages 8–14

Now in an updated second edition, *How to Teach Writing Across the Curriculum: Ages 8–14* provides a range of practical suggestions for teaching non-fiction writing skills and linking them to students' learning across the curriculum. Emphasising creative approaches to teaching writing in diverse and innovative ways, it provides:

- information on the organisation and language features of the six main non-fiction text types (recount, report, instruction, explanation, persuasion and discussion);
- suggestions for the use of cross-curricular learning as a basis for writing;
- planning frameworks for students to use;
- advice on developing students' writing to help with organisational issues – paragraphing and layout, and the key language features;
- examples of non-fiction writing;
- suggestions for talk for learning and talk for writing (including links to *Speaking Frames*, also published by Routledge);
- information on the transition from primary to secondary school.

With new hints and tips for teachers and suggestions for reflective practice as well as a wealth of photocopiable materials, *How to Teach Writing Across the Curriculum: Ages 8–14* will equip teachers with all the skills needed to create enthusiastic non-fiction writers in their classroom.

**Sue Palmer** is a writer, broadcaster and education consultant. Specialising in the teaching of literacy, she has authored over 150 books and has contributed to numerous television programmes and software packages. She is the author of *Speaking Frames: How to Teach Talk for Writing: Ages 8–10* and *Speaking Frames: How to Teach Talk for Writing: Ages 10–14*, also published by Routledge.

**Also available in the Writers' Workshop Series:**

*How to Teach Writing Across the Curriculum: Ages 6–8*
Sue Palmer
(ISBN: 978-0-415-57990-2)

# How to Teach Writing Across the Curriculum: Ages 8–14

## Second edition

## Sue Palmer

Routledge
Taylor & Francis Group
LONDON AND NEW YORK

First edition published as *How to Teach Writing Across the Curriculum at Key Stage 2*
by David Fulton Publishers 2001

This edition published 2011
by Routledge
2 Park Square, Milton Park, Abingdon, Oxon, OX14 4RN

Simultaneously published in the USA and Canada
by Routledge
270 Madison Avenue, New York, NY 10016

*Routledge is an imprint of the Taylor & Francis Group, an informa business*

© 2011 Sue Palmer

Typeset in Helvetica by FiSH Books
Printed and bound in Great Britain by MPG Books Group, UK

*British Library Cataloguing in Publication Data*
A catalogue record for this book is available from the British Library

*Library of Congress Cataloging-in-Publication Data*
Palmer, Sue, 1948–
How to teach writing across the curriculum : ages 8–14 / Sue Palmer. — 2nd ed.
    p. cm.
1. Language arts (Elementary)—Great Britain. 2. Language arts (Secondary)—Great Britain. 3. Language arts—Correlation with content subjects—Great Britain. 4. English language—Writing—Study and teaching (Elementary)—Great Britain. 5. English language—Study and teaching (Secondary)—Great Britain. 6. Curriculum planning—Great Britain. I. Title.
LB1576.P255 2011
428.0071—dc22

2010006349

ISBN13: 978-0-415-57991-9 (pbk)
ISBN13: 978-0-203-84579-0 (ebk)

# Contents

# Introduction: teaching writing

Some years ago I was on *Woman's Hour*. It was a debate about the relative importance of 'old and new literacies', and I'd been invited along as the representative of a bygone age to talk about reading and writing. My fellow debater was an ICT specialist called Dr Chris Yapp, who advises government on the skills today's children will need when they eventually enter the workforce.

At the time, I was besotted with information technology. When asked what I thought of 'new literacies' I launched into an enthusiastic speech about how computers could make the learning of basic skills much more fun, and how wonderful multimedia is for cross-curricular learning.

It was a bit of a surprise when Dr Yapp cut across me with the words, 'Yes that's all very well, but the children have to be able to read properly first.'

He then explained that in the future computer keyboards will only be used for instructions – indeed keyboards may fade completely away as touch-screen technology develops. The main way we'll input information into our computers will be via voice-activated software (this is already increasingly the case in high-tech offices). So to prepare children to speak clearly and grammatically into voice-activated software, they need to practise reading aloud.

I drove home from the broadcast frantically considering the implications of Dr Yapp's prediction. If adults of the future will seldom actually write anything down, how should today's teachers teach writing skills? Will they be seen as increasingly less important, and attention turn more and more to the teaching of speaking and listening?

It's due to several years' engagement with this issue that this new edition of *How to Teach Writing Across the Curriculum* has a different emphasis (and a very different teaching model) from the earlier one. Discussion with colleagues from many disciplines convinces me that any advice on writing should begin with in-depth discussion about the differences between writing and speech.

## From speech to writing

The critical – and enormous – difference between the two uses of language is that human beings are hard-wired for speech. As long as they listen to plenty of talk and song in their earliest years, and have opportunities to copy the sounds and words they hear, they'll start to talk themselves. And if that talk is nurtured through interaction with adults and other children, they'll eventually become fluent speakers.

But that doesn't mean they'll necessarily become fluent writers. As one loquacious ten-year-old told me, when I asked him why speaking is so much easier than writing, 'Well, when you talk, you don't have to think about it. You just open your mouth and the words sort of flow out...But when you write...erm, you have to get a pencil, and you have to get a piece of paper, and then...and then...and then you feel really tired.'

I know lots of talkative children who feel really tired when confronted with a pencil and paper. The trouble is that human beings aren't hard-wired for literacy. Reading and writing are cultural constructs, and each new generation has to be taught – painstakingly, and over several years – how words can be turned into squiggly symbols on paper. What's more, the language of writing is very different from the natural language patterns of speech.

Speech is generally interactive – we bat words and phrases back and forth. It's produced within a shared context, so it's fragmented, disorganised and a great deal of meaning goes by on the nod. In fact, you can get by in speech without ever forming a sentence, or at least only very simple ones. To make links between ideas, speakers tend to use very simple connectives, like the ubiquitous *and* or, to denote sequence, *and then.*

Nowadays, in a world in which images are increasingly taking over from words, speech has become even less specific. Gesture, facial expression and tone of voice are often used instead of verbal description (for instance: '*And I was feeling like – Whaaat?*' where '*Whaaat?*' is pronounced in a tone of exaggerated disbelief, accompanied by an expression of wide-eyed incredulity.)

But written language is produced for an unknown, unseen audience, who may have no background knowledge at all about the subject. It must therefore be explicit and carefully crafted. It requires more extensive vocabulary than speech and organisation into sentences for clarity. The sentences become increasingly complex as the writer expresses increasingly complex ideas, using a widening range of connectives to show how these ideas relate to each other. Written language has to have its own internal cohesion.

So the mental effort involved in writing is immeasurably greater than that involved in speaking. It's not just a case of working out what you want to say without the benefit of body language, facial expression, voice tone and a shared context. You also have to translate it into a much more complex, utterly unnatural language code – different vocabulary, different sentence structures, the challenge of making a whole text hold together and make sense.

## Learning to write

Even experienced writers usually recognise exactly what that ten-year-old guru meant. Indeed, as a professional writer for 25 years, I regularly go into my office, switch on the computer, and when the screen lights up – all blank and scary – find myself muttering '*I'll just go and make a cup of tea.*'

For apprentice writers, the task is even more complex and daunting. As well as struggling to convey meaning in an unfamiliar code, they simultaneously have to:

1 Remember how words are composed of sounds, and wrestle with the exigencies of our spelling system. That means (a) applying what they know about phonics and (b) remembering which of many common English words don't actually follow phonic rules.
2 Manipulate a pencil across a page, or their fingers across a keyboard, while keeping the whole thing going as neatly and speedily as possible.
3 Keep in mind all the conventions of written texts – sentence punctuation, the sorts of sentence construction and vocabulary appropriate to different tasks, paragraphing and other aspects of cohesion.

4  Remember, and organize into some sort of sense, the factual content of whatever it is they're writing about.

Learning to write is probably the most complex and challenging academic task most human beings undertake in their whole lives. What's more, despite the immense amount of mental (and physical) effort involved, the rewards in the early stages are often minimal while the potential for failure is great. So it's all too easy for motivation to grind to a halt.

It's not surprising, then, that after several decades of intense effort on behalf of the teaching profession – with government initiatives and targets galore – writing is still a problem area. Children who lose motivation through repeated failure can begin to feel so 'tired' about the whole business, that they're never able to summon up the effort to become fluent writers.

## Why writing matters

Yet becoming a fluent writer is still – even in an age of multimedia and speech-activated software – extraordinarily important. Research for my books on child development in the modern world[1] (inspired in part by Dr Yapp's remark) has convinced me that, as screen-based communication and entertainment proliferate, learning to write is an even more critical element in the development of children's thinking skills.

As mentioned earlier, spoken language is spontaneous – you don't have to think about what you say before you say it – while written language must be carefully crafted. It requires *conscious control* on behalf of the writer. This capacity to control behaviour and thought processes is the mark of a civilised, educated brain. And increasing control of language (vocabulary, sentence structure, linking ideas together) underpins many aspects of rational thought. So, from a young child's first faltering efforts to spell out *The cat sat on the mat* to a university student's ability to compose an essay, developing skill as writer helps make him or her become more educated, civilised and rational.

Neuroscientists have found that literacy 'changes the architecture of the brain'. The human capacity for reading and writing not only allows us to record our ideas, and thus share our developing understanding of the world over time and space. It also creates massively enriched neural networks inside the skulls of each and every one of us. It changes our minds.

For an apprentice writer, learning to rally all those writing sub-skills means orchestrating activity in many areas of the brain – a huge mental task (no wonder they feel tired). As their basic competence grows, the physical act of writing means children must slow down their thought processes, giving time to consider the language itself. *How can I best express this idea? How can I make the links between one idea and the next?* Once ideas are pinned down on a page, the writer can refine or revise them – finding links, explaining underlying connections (and perhaps exploring them further), developing arguments.

What's more, as students steadily acquire the literate vocabulary and sentence structures needed to write well, this more sophisticated language can feed into their speech, and gradually they become able to talk in literate language patterns too. Literacy is about a great deal more than reading and writing – it's about the way people think and speak and (since it helps develop self control) even how they act.

## Teaching writing across the curriculum

So as school students become increasingly well-versed in the basics of writing, and able to record their learning across the curriculum, their language capacity is linked to their overall potential to learn. Teaching writing across the curriculum involves bringing together many higher order literacy and learning skills. We have to help students:

- acquire and internalise the factual content to be recorded;
- organise that factual content for their own purposes;
- consider the audience and specific purpose of the text – how much detail will my readers require? Is the intention to inform, persuade, explain, instruct...?;
- select appropriate layout and language to convey the content appropriately.

It's a hugely complex and important task.

Over the last quarter century, I've wrestled with the question of how teachers can simultaneously cover subject matter, reasons for writing, layout, language *and* the multitudinous secretarial skills required to put it all down on paper. And I've come firmly to the opinion that those secretarial skills (specific elements of grammar, handwriting and spelling) must be taught separately from content. The human brain can't concentrate on both meaning and the conscious processing of technicalities at the same time.

Mind you, I suspect it won't be all that long before the nuts and bolts of 'word level' and 'sentence level' writing skills are seen as irrelevant beyond the age of about nine. Automatic spellcheckers, grammatical autocorrects and voice activated software will make anything more than the rudiments of 'pencil and paper writing' unnecessary. We'll have more time to concentrate on techniques to clarify meaning, from punctuation and paragraphing to connectives and other cohesive vocabulary. In the meantime, secretarial skills should be dealt with away from purposeful writing contexts. (I'd recommend short, punchy lessons such as those suggested by Pie Corbett in his book *Jumpstart! Literacy.*[2])

Cross-curricular writing is about the four bullet points at the beginning of this section, with ideas and information acquired across the curriculum providing the subject-matter to be recorded. And at all points in the process, it's also about the interface between spoken and written language. This begins with recognising the importance of learners' natural spoken language in learning and organising content before writing. It then involves hijacking natural learning strategies to help young writers internalise the literate language patterns they need to write fluently. We need to develop 'talk for learning' and 'talk for writing'.

## Subject teaching and English teaching

By the time children are about eight years old, they're relatively skilled at spoken language and have usually acquired the basic nuts and bolts of written language: handwriting, spelling (phonetically regular and common irregular words) and written sentence construction. Over the next half dozen years, they need to refine their skill in using language to explore, express and record their learning across the curriculum.

When a 'class teacher' is responsible for covering the whole curriculum – as is usually the case in primary schools – it's relatively easy to link cross-curricular learning and literacy skills. But as specialist teachers take over responsibility for specific areas of the curriculum, there's a widening gulf between subject knowledge (e.g. history, geography, science) and English teaching.

This book shows how to make links between learning across the curriculum and the teaching of literacy. Since English teachers have major responsibility for literacy development, the book is primarily aimed at them. But subject specialists are also responsible for developing 'key skills' relevant to their fields of study – so they too need to be aware of significant aspects of non-fiction writing. The relevant elements are described in the 'two horses model' for teaching writing (and especially the skeleton system of recording understanding) described in the next section.

Broadly speaking, if subject specialists cover the 'top horse' in the model ('Talk for Learning'), English teachers can use students' cross-curricular learning to develop the 'bottom horse' ('Talk for Writing'), and show how to convert that learning into written language. If English teachers can convince colleagues of the value of following the model, there are clear advantages for all teachers and students – not least in terms of time spent on recording students' learning. Brief notes and handouts are provided in Appendix 1 to help bring non-English specialists on board.

Fortunately, the 'two horses model' and 'skeletons' are both immensely simple concepts. In my inservice work, I've found teachers across all age ranges immediately see their application, and have no difficulty applying it as most appropriate to their own classes' needs. Indeed, in one glorious week I saw the same 'skeleton' materials in use in a nursery school and at Oxford University! I suspect it's because the ideas are rooted in ways of thinking and using language that come naturally to human beings, whether they are teachers or learners. The all-important role of teachers is to apply them in ways that work best for whatever it is they have to teach.

### *References*

1 *Toxic Childhood* (2006), *Detoxing Childhood* (2007), *21st Century Boys* (2009) and *21st Century Girls* (2011) by Sue Palmer, all published by Orion Books.
2 *Jumpstart! Literacy* (2004) by Pie Corbett, published by David Fulton.

# PART 1

# The two horses model for cross-curricular literacy

*You can't teach children to write before they can talk. It's putting the cart before the horse.*

It's over a decade now since a teacher in Yorkshire uttered those words at one of my inservice courses. As I drove home that night I started wondering exactly how teachers could ensure that the 'horse' of talk was properly hitched up to draw the 'cart' of writing.

Eventually, after long conversations with many colleagues (especially my fellow literacy consultant Pie Corbett), I concluded that, in order to write, students need two sorts of talk:

- talk for learning – plenty of opportunities to use the simple spontaneous language of speech to ensure they understand the ideas and content they're going to write about;
- talk for writing – opportunities to meet and internalise the relevant patterns of 'literate language', to help them turn that content into well-crafted sentences.

So students need not one but two 'horses' to draw the writing 'cart':

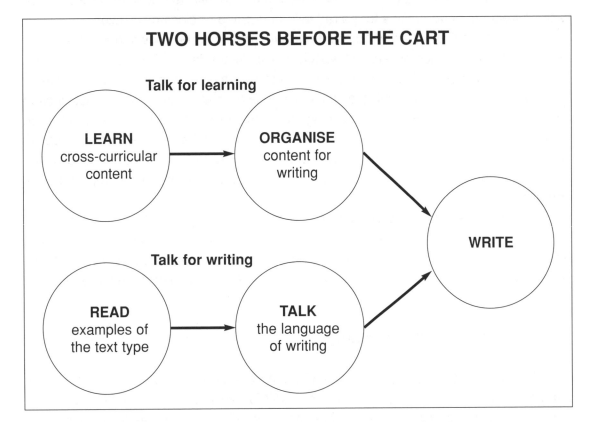

**Figure 1.1** A teaching plan for cross-curricular literacy (simple form)

# 1.1 Talk for learning

## Learn cross-curricular content

In order to understand the content of cross-curricular teaching, apprentice writers need – just as they have always needed – plenty of opportunities for talk. These are provided through the sort of 'active learning' that provides opportunities for speaking and listening, such as:

- opportunities for imaginative engagement – drama, role-play, 'hot-seating';
- outings, excursions, field trips and other opportunities to find out about the wider world through experience and talk to a range of adults;
- active engagement in learning whenever possible: experimenting, making pictures, models, collages, websites, 'TV documentaries' etc (there are now so many ways of creating audio and video records of learning activities);
- audio-visual aids for learning – for instance, relevant items to look at, touch and talk about;
- storytelling – listening to adults telling stories and anecdotes, and having opportunities to tell them themselves;
- responding to ideas through music, movement, art and craft.

Of course, in addition, students need opportunities to talk about and around ideas, through frequent opportunities for paired talk, and group or class discussion.

Such opportunities for active, motivating learning should be provided in all areas of the curriculum, whether by subject specialists in secondary school or by the class teacher in top primary. With so much attention these days to 'pencil and paper' work, it is sometimes tempting to think that they're a waste of valuable time. In fact, they're essential not only for learning, but for language and literacy development – and they're the obvious way to make the best use of cross-curricular links to literacy. When subject specialists collaborate with English teachers in this way to help students develop the ideas, concepts, vocabulary and excitement that underpins good writing, everyone benefits.

Experience has shown that certain types of active learning sit particularly comfortably with the different text types we use for cross-curricular writing, as shown in the boxes below. These activities reflect the underlying structures of thought upon which the text types depend, and thus link to the planning skeletons described in the next section.

## Organise content for learning

The different text types are characterised by their underlying structures – i.e. the ways that particular types of information are organised for writing. Awareness of these structures can become a powerful aid to understanding, allowing students to organise their learning in the form of notes or pictures before – or **instead of** – writing.

### *Skeletons for writing*

I originally devised the 'skeleton' frameworks shown in the box for the English National Literacy Strategy. At the time, we called them 'graphic organisers' or 'diagrammatic representations', neither of which was a snappy title to use with primary children. It was a boy in the north east of England who christened them. He rushed up to his teacher with the words: 'They're skeletons, aren't they, Miss? They're the skeletons that you hang the writing on!' Thanks to that unknown Geordie lad, the skeleton frameworks became instantly memorable.

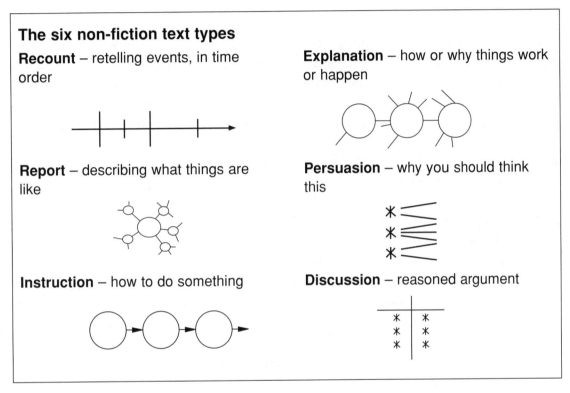

**Figure 1.1.1** A range of skeletons

Since then, extensive work by teachers across the UK has shown that the use of skeleton planning frameworks can pay off in many ways.

### *A range of skeletons*

The skeleton frameworks shown above are intended to be representative of each of the text types. As such they provide a visual 'icon' which reminds students of the structure of the text:

- A **timeline** icon was chosen to represent recount because it is a simple, clear indicator of chronological order (using left → right as an indicator of time passing), and visually easy to remember.
- The **simple flowchart** icon for instructions demonstrates sequence in the same way, but the circles suggest a number of discrete steps or stages in the process.

- In contrast, the **spidergram** icon shows clearly that chronology is not involved in writing report text: here the visual display suggests a basic central concept from which radiates information organised into categories.
- The **complex flowchart** icon indicates that explanations are usually sequential but that there is further contributory detail at each stage: here the sequence involves cause and effect.
- The **pronged bullet** icon for persuasive writing suggests that the key to organisation is the arranging of arguments into a number of major points, each of which requires elaboration in the form of evidence or further background information.
- A **for-and-against grid** suggests that discussion text involves the organisation of points and elaboration on both sides of an argument.

Experience suggests that it is best to use a particular skeleton icon as a planning framework when students are still familiarising themselves with a text type, to help them internalise the underlying structure. However, there are many other ways in which each text type might be represented, and as time goes on students should also be encouraged to recognise these and choose the one that best suits any individual occasion, e.g.:

- The sequential, chronological structure of **recount** and **instructions** could be represented by a story-board, a flow chart, a calendar or clock face diagram, or simply a numbered list.
- A very simple **report** might be better represented by a labelled picture or diagram; comparative reports often require a grid skeleton.
- **Explanation** text sometimes requires multiple cause–effect boxes or a cyclical structure (see page 70), or may sometimes be represented by a diagram or sequence of diagrams – in fact, creating graphic representations of the structures underlying individual explanation texts is an excellent way of helping students develop their understanding of cause and effect.
- **Persuasion** text could be represented on a spidergram, and discussion text on a double spidergram.

As students become familiar with the idea of skeletons, their repertoire of graphic representations can be gradually enlarged.

### How to use skeletons

Skeleton planning provides a link between cross-curricular content and specific teaching of writing skills. All teachers (whether or not they're responsible for literacy teaching) can introduce students to these ways of organising ideas by:

- demonstrating how to use skeletons themselves as simple note-taking devices and aide-memoires throughout the curriculum;
- teaching students how to draw the skeletons, and recognise which sorts of ideas and texts are associated with each skeleton;
- sending skeleton notes to the literacy lesson, so they can be used to link knowledge and understanding acquired in a wide range of subject areas with the literacy skills required to record that understanding.

Debbie Billard, a teacher in Rotherham, coined the term 'memory-joggers' for the jottings on a skeleton framework. She explains that memory-joggers are not proper sentences, nor do they have to be words at all. Notes, diagrams, symbols, pictures and photographs are all acceptable – anything that will jog the memory when one comes to write.

The skeleton can then be used like a carrier bag to bring this cross-curricular content to the literacy or English lesson. Once students have been taught the relevant language features of recount text, they can use their memory-joggers to write. Debbie's suggestion is to 'turn your memory-joggers into sentences'.

Teachers who have used skeleton frameworks with their classes have pointed out a number of advantages:

- Making skeleton notes helps students organise what they have learned to aid memorisation of the facts.
- Many students (especially boys) find it helpful to make this kind of 'big picture' record, so they have an overview of the whole piece of writing before beginning to write (which is, by its nature, a linear sequential process, rather than a holistic one).
- Today's students are highly visually literate and skeleton records help them use visual memory skills to aid learning.
- As students learn a repertoire of skeletons, they can use them to take notes for a variety of purposes, not just as a precursor to writing.
- Skeletons allow teachers and students to make clear links between literacy skills and the rest of the curriculum.
- Planning on a skeleton allows students to organise the content of their writing in advance (including dividing material into sections and paragraphing) – it means that when they actually settle down to write, they can concentrate entirely on the language of writing.
- Making a skeleton with the class provides an opportunity for highly focused speaking and listening.
- Making a skeleton with a partner is an excellent focus for paired talk.
- Using skeletons develops students' thinking skills.

It seems clear from talking to teachers that skeletons have the potential to be more than simple recording or planning devices for writing. Perhaps the most exciting suggestion is that skeleton planning can become a way of developing generic thinking skills – helping students recognise the different ways human beings organise their ideas, depending on the subject matter we're addressing. In the case studies in *How to Teach Writing Across the Curriculum: Ages 6–8*, teachers have shown that, through using these visual models, even very young children can grapple with the structures that underlie thought and language.

## Recount skeletons

Recount writing is often seen as the easiest non-fiction text type to teach, since recounts are organised chronologically, like a story. There are many occasions when students have a 'true story' to write, e.g.:

- accounts of schoolwork or outings;
- stories from history or RE;
- anecdotes and personal accounts;
- biographical writing in any curricular area.

However, chronological writing is not without its pitfalls. All teachers are familiar with accounts of school trips that deal admirably with the bus journey but omit to mention what happened later on. Some students, even at secondary level, have difficulty ordering events appropriately in historical or biographical accounts.

Most students therefore benefit from organising the facts on a timeline before writing. This provides:

- an opportunity to sort out the main events, and their sequence, without the added mental effort of putting them into sentences;
- an overview of **all** the events, in clear chronological order, so the author knows exactly how much he or she has to cover (and doesn't get stuck on the bus);
- an opportunity to consider how to divide the information into paragraphs **before** beginning to write;
- an opportunity to decide whether to follow a linear chronological structure or to adapt the time sequence for effect, e.g. starting with a key event in a biography.

## Instruction skeletons

It's usually tricky explaining how to do something unless you've done it yourself first. When professional writers work out instructions for recipes or craft activities, they usually create a rough plan, then work through the process – amending and adding to their notes and diagrams as they go along – before writing it up carefully for publication. In order for students to write clear instructions, they too usually need first-hand experience of the process concerned.

There are many occasions across the curriculum when students carry out activities which can become the content for writing instructions, e.g.:

- designing and making an artefact in DT;
- procedures for operating the computer in ICT;
- science experiments;
- art activities;
- dances or games in PE;
- general classroom procedures;
- procedures in maths.

If students are encouraged to adopt the professionals' approach, their on-going notes or annotated plans for the activity can double as 'skeleton notes' for instruction writing. If, as a result of their first hand experience, they are then secure about the content of their instructions, this leaves them free to concentrate on the language features and layout of the particular instruction text type whilst writing.

## Report skeletons

There are many occasions across the curriculum when students need to learn about the **characteristics** of something – what it is (or was) like.

These include:

- **history**, e.g. aspects of daily life in any historical period;
- **science**, e.g. characteristics, general life patterns and habitats of plants and animals;
- **geography**, e.g. descriptions of localities and geographical features.

The problem with such information is that it does not always have an immediately obvious organisational structure, like the chronological sequence of a story. Before they can talk or write about the topic succinctly, students must find ways of organising the facts coherently.

A note-making 'skeleton' such as a spidergram can help them organise their thoughts and clarify understanding of what they have learned. These diagrammatic notes can also form a bridge between the wider curriculum and literacy, providing the content for **non-chronological report** writing.

The organisation of information on a skeleton framework can help students see how facts can be clustered. It can also clarify how best to divide their text into sections and/or paragraphs.

## Explanation skeleton

Sometimes language can be an inadequate tool for explaining how something works. In spoken language situations, adults often find themselves scrabbling for a pencil to draw a diagram – so they can point and indicate movement and direction alongside the verbal explanation ('The electric current goes round here and through here . . . ').

Many students need help in learning how to integrate the visual and the verbal in technical explanations. Opportunities occur throughout the curriculum, for instance:

- **history**, e.g. Roman road-building; organisation of social systems, steam locomotion;
- **science**, e.g. electricity; the seasons; insulation; any scientific experiment;
- **geography**, e.g. the water cycle; how a volcano erupts.

When such occasions arise, it's important to draw attention to the main characteristics of various types of diagram (e.g. plans, maps and cross-sections) and 'skeleton' note-taking frameworks (flow charts and picture sequences).

Students can be encouraged to devise their own diagrams and skeleton notes which can be used in a literacy lesson as content for explanatory writing. As in spoken language, however, a purely written account is often inadequate: students must learn to integrate diagrams and flowcharts with the written word to ensure their explanations are truly effective.

## Persuasion skeletons

School students are bombarded daily with persuasive texts: advertisements, magazine articles, brochures, leaflets, fliers. Writing such texts for themselves helps develop awareness of the techniques others use to influence their thinking. However, in order to persuade someone else to your point of view, you must first be knowledgeable about your subject matter.

There are many cross-curricular opportunities for persuasive writing:

- **history,** e.g. a local history study or visit to a museum can provide background information for a publicity campaign and brochure;
- **science**, e.g. knowledge about teeth, nutrition, drug abuse can be used in compiling leaflets, posters or articles promoting a healthy lifestyle;
- **geography**, e.g. students can express their own viewpoints on topics 'In the News' or local issues, such as 'Should the High Street be closed to traffic?';
- **PHSE and citizenship** e.g. students could devise campaigns about bullying, road safety, aspects of civic responsibility, etc.

To argue their case in writing, students must select and organise information, usually as a series of major points, each of which may require elaboration (explanation, evidence and/or examples). Notes on a 'skeleton' framework can help with this organisation. Students are then free when writing to concentrate on the language features of persuasive text.

## Discussion skeletons

Throughout the curriculum – and, indeed, throughout their lives – students will encounter issues on which there is more than one viewpoint, often fiercely-held opinions. Writing discussion texts introduces them to techniques for reaching a balanced assessment of the matter in hand, so they avoid making rapid, uninformed judgements.

Controversies may arise, for instance, in:

- **history**, e.g. historical attitudes to race, gender, children, class, colonialism;
- **RE**, e.g. fundamentalism, religious intolerance;
- **geography**, e.g. pollution, effects of development;
- **science**, e.g. space exploration, aspects of diet;
- **PHSE,** e.g. bullying, substance abuse.

Controversy also regularly raises its head during the reading of fiction, where students' opinions on an issue may be affected by the viewpoint of a particular character.

One way of helping them see more than one point of view is to compile a simple for-and-against grid during class discussion. Apart from the valuable intellectual exercise of listing points on both sides of an argument, this also provides a reason for students to express their arguments as succinctly as possible – to be condensed into intelligible notes for the grid. The grid can also bring issues from any area of the curriculum to a literacy lesson, where teaching can focus on text organisation and language features.

# 1.2 Talk for writing

Once students securely understand the content they are to write about, they need help in acquiring appropriate language structures to express it. As is shown on pages 38, 50, 62, 70, 78 and 86 each of the text types is characterised by certain language features. The teaching of cross-curricular writing therefore provides many opportunities for revisiting aspects of grammar within a purposeful writing context.

However, care should always be taken not to *over-focus* on grammatical or stylistic elements at the expense of meaning. This is why 'word' and 'sentence' level teaching are best covered separately from meaningful writing tasks. Shared Writing then provides an opportunity to illustrate how these elements are used in writing, referring to them briefly and tangentially without interfering with the overall flow.

It's also important that students' own assessment of their work should not be a mere exercise in box-ticking against a checklist of language features. When teaching focuses on the bureaucracy of learning at the expense of the meaningful whole, there's a price to pay in students' motivation, understanding and – in the long run – ability to write (and think) well and fluently.

## Read examples of the text type

Reading, in any aspect of literacy, should always precede writing. Every teacher knows that students who read lots of fiction for pleasure tend also to be good at writing fiction – they absorb the rhythms and patterns of narrative language through repeated exposure. They also pick up new vocabulary by meeting it in context. Nowadays however, with the ready availability of screen-based entertainment, fewer students see the point of reading for pleasure, so fewer of them tend to be 'natural' storytellers.

This has, in fact, always been the case with non-fiction writing. The non-fiction text types described in the previous section have various textual characteristics with which writers need to be familiar, but only the most voracious readers of non-fiction are likely to be familiar with them (and then, usually, only in limited genres).

### Listen > imitate > innovate > invent

It's worth going back to first principles and working out how children acquire new forms of language from their earliest days. If we then apply these principles to the acquisition of 'literate language' patterns, perhaps we can compensate for lack of experience in reading. (And if we're really lucky, perhaps our efforts can turn some students on to more reading for themselves, too.)

Babies learn to speak by **listening** to the adults around them, and **imitating** the sounds they hear. This involves tuning into the phonemes of the language, and much baby babble is practise of these individual sounds – 'bababababa', 'dadadada', 'gagagaga', and so on. But they also imitate the patterns and rhythms of speech, babbling away in response to adult language, so it often sounds as if they're joining in the conversation with their nonsense talk. As babies and toddlers are exposed to more and more spoken language, they start picking up whole words and phrases and imitating them. Gradually, through the miracle of human language acquisition, they work out how to **innovate** on the language patterns they hear, and finally **invent** whole speeches for themselves.

Children from educated homes are also frequently exposed to 'literate language' patterns, partly because their parents read to them from an early age, but also because the adult language going on around them day-by-day is pretty literate too. These students are at a huge advantage at school, because they're already familiar with the vocabulary and language structures of writing. But teachers can ensure that all students in the class get as many opportunities as possible to listen, imitate, innovate and invent along literate lines – and the younger we start work on this, the better chance we'd have of levelling the playing field a little for students from disadvantaged backgrounds.

### Reading aloud

The most obvious way to expose all students to literate language patterns is to read well-written non-fiction aloud – magazine and blog articles, short sections from text books, and so on. This helps familiarise them – via their ears – with the vocabulary and language patterns of the text types. As Robert Louis Stevenson put it, this is an excellent way of sensitising young minds to *'the chime of fine words and the march of the stately period'*.

Another excellent strategy is to provide opportunities for students to read non-fiction texts aloud themselves. This gives them the chance to hear literate language patterns produced from their own mouths; to know how standard English and sophisticated vocabulary *feels*; to respond physically to the ebb and flow of well-constructed sentences, learning incidentally how punctuation guides meaning and expression. There's a pay-off in both speech and writing when we let accomplished authors put words into our students' mouths.

Reading aloud has acquired a bad reputation in recent years. The traditional technique of 'reading round the class' is embarrassing for poor readers and excruciatingly boring for good ones. But there are other ways of giving students opportunities to read decent texts aloud.

One is **paired reading**, when two students share a book or short text, dividing the reading between them. Depending on their level of ability, this could be alternate pages or alternate paragraphs. (For special needs students, reading alternate sentences encourages them to look for the full stops, and thus take note of sentence boundaries.)

When the class needs some subject knowledge, paired reading of a text is a good way to provide it.

Another is **reader's theatre**, when a group of students are asked to prepare an oral presentation of a short text for the rest of the class. There's no room here to describe it at length, but you'll find plenty of details and good ideas on internet search engines.

## Talk the language of writing

### Speaking frames

We can also provide opportunities for students to innovate on written language patterns by creating 'speaking frames' for the sorts of vocabulary and sentence structures we want them to produce in their writing.

Below is a completed speaking frame using the language of comparison. Students were asked in groups to find four points of comparison between two disparate objects (it could have been two locations, historical characters, books, films, or anything else). Having agreed their points in discussion, they divided them up to report back to the class on the frame, given in bold:

> **There are several ways in which** a glass tumbler **and** a shoe **could be said to be similar.**
>
> **The first way they are both alike is that they are both** containers. The glass is a container for liquids and the shoe is a container for someone's foot.
>
> **Another similarity is that they** are man-made. Both are manufactured in factories, and sold in shops.
>
> **A further feature they have in common is** that they are solid objects. However, a glass is transparent and a shoe is usually opaque.
>
> **Finally they both** need regular cleaning. A glass must be washed after use, and a shoe needs polishing to keep it looking good.
>
> **We think the most significant similarity is that** they are containers, because this is their function.

If several groups report back on the frame, this activity gives an opportunity to repeat the first three stages of **listen > imitate > innovate > invent** several times.

- **listen**: they hear key phrases and vocabulary read aloud several times during each group's feedback;
- **imitate**: they speak some language patterns aloud as they complete their section of the speaking frame;
- **innovate**: they hear/create innovations by completing the frame.

Often we expect students to go straight to the 'inventing' stage in writing with little or no opportunity to internalise language structures through the experiences of the earlier stages. It is therefore worth looking for ways to integrate the **listen > imitate > innovate > invent** sequence into day-by-day teaching to familiarise students with written language patterns (including sentence constructions), and to allow them the experience of producing, from their own mouths, more sophisticated language than they would usually use.

Using a 'speaking frame' can be a regular part of shared work. If more able students report back on a speaking frame first, the less able have the opportunity to hear it several times before it comes to their turn. *Speaking Frames: How to Teach Talk for*

*Writing* (*8–10* and *10–14*) is a companion series to this book, providing many examples of speaking frames for individual, paired and group work, and 'smorgasbords' of literate language for students and teachers to make their own frames.

### Sentence level work

As mentioned above, word and sentence level teaching should be covered away from the act of writing. In terms of teaching text types, sentence level teaching should be very light-touch, and – as far as possible – should engage students in active investigation of language.

This usually begins with **shared reading** of examples of a particular text type and talk about how authors express their ideas. Students can then be sent off to collect examples of the sorts of language they use from other similar texts, e.g.:

- time connectives in recount;
- imperative verbs in instructions;
- the use of examples in report;
- causal language structures in explanation;
- the language of generalisation in persuasion;
- ways of clearly stating opposing views in discussion.

Students can be alerted to grammatical patterns through:

- oral games (e.g. changing verbs into the past tense);
- class collections of words and phrases (e.g. posters for time connectives, ways of conveying cause-and-effect words; banks of useful adjectives, etc.);
- focused speaking and listening activities in which students create sentences of their own, featuring the appropriate language features (e.g. see Speaking frames, above).

The key to all these activities is plenty of opportunity to be actively engaged, especially in speaking and listening. Sometimes it's possible to do this as a class, but more often the solution is paired work.

### Paired work

Each student is allocated a 'talking partner' – someone with whom they can be trusted to work well. Whenever the opportunity arises you say: 'Turn to your partner. You have 30 seconds [or two minutes, or whatever] to discuss . . .' Selected pairs can then retell their deliberations to the class.

Teachers who have used this system effectively stress the importance of training and careful organization in the early stages:

- One student can work as the teacher's partner to model the appropriate behaviour, then the class splits into pairs to try it. There should also be opportunities to discuss the point of the exercise, and good and bad points of procedure.
- Snippets from training videos can also be useful for showing the class how the system works.

However, once the system is up and running, it can become a regular part of classroom life. Robin Alexander's book *Towards Dialogic Teaching* (Dialogos, 2008) illustrates how throwing ideas to students for discussion in pairs provides far greater opportunities for them to engage with ideas, to use technical vocabulary, and thus to internalize learning.

For special needs students, talking partners can also double as 'writing partners', allowing them to take advantage of oral rehearsal and oral revision of their work.

Our 'two horses' model for cross-curricular writing now looks like this:

**TWO HORSES BEFORE THE CART**

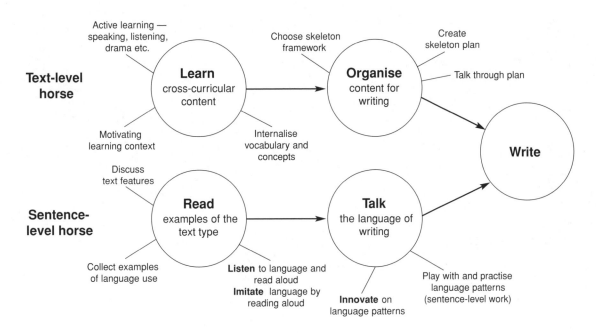

**Figure 1.2.1** Two horses before the cart

# PART 2
# Case studies

# 2.1 Recount case study

### Learn cross-curricular content

The content for writing in this project came when the teacher told his class of eleven-year-olds the story of Gandhi, bringing an RE dimension to a project on 'Great Lives'. With their help, he created a timeline representation of this story on a long strip of wallpaper. The students then dramatised Gandhi's life-story in groups, each group focusing on a different period and creating a short play for performance to the class.

The students sat around the hall, and the teacher 'put the spotlight' on each group in turn to create a complete performance. He then rolled the timeline up and left it in a cupboard for a week or so.

### Organise ideas

On this occasion, the making of skeleton notes had already been done as a class, when the teacher drew the timeline. The class had also broken it into paragraphs (by drawing vertical lines) when deciding on the sections to be acted out. When the time came to focus on writing, the teacher retrieved the skeleton from the cupboard.

## Talk for writing

### Read examples of the text type

The class had been reading about other major figures in world religions. In literacy lessons, they studied some examples of this biographical writing (especially encyclopaedia entries), focusing particularly on:

- major language features, including past tense and variation in sentence structure;
- characteristics of the opening and concluding sentences in each paragraph.

The teacher then brought Gandhi's skeleton out of the cupboard and demonstrated, in a Shared Writing session, how to expand one paragraph into recount writing ('turn your memory-joggers into sentences'):

> As a member of the Indian National Congress, Mahatma Gandhi did everything he could to help poor people in the villages. They were taught first aid, hygiene and crafts like making cloth by hand. Gandhi disapproved of machines because he believed they took work from the poor. He had learned to spin and weave himself, and made the fabric for his own simple clothing.

### Talk the language of writing

The teacher asked students, in pairs, to use the skeleton notes to retell the story of Gandhi to each other, a paragraph each. This gave them the opportunity to develop a verbal narrative – using, wherever possible, the type of literate language patterns they'd been studying. It was also a chance to discover which bits they were unsure of – to fill in any gaps they could either:

- ask the teacher or actors from the relevant group;
- check them up in reference books or on the web.

### Write

The writing up of the recount was shared between the class. Each pair of students worked on one paragraph (including an introductory paragraph summarising why Gandhi was famous), and the class selected the most successful pieces of writing to be combined into a complete biography. This was edited to ensure cohesion and flow between the paragraphs and produced on the computer for inclusion in the class's display on 'Great Lives'.

Each student now chose a hero or heroine to research and write about, using the model demonstrated for their work on Gandhi:

- create a timeline;
- divide it into sections;
- expand each section into a paragraph to create a complete piece of biographical recount writing.

# 2.2 Report case study

### Learn cross-curricular content

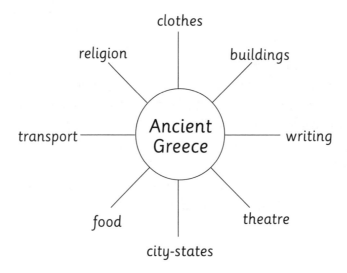

**Figure 2.2.1** Ancient Greece spidergram

For a history project, pairs of eleven-year-old students were asked to choose and research one topic from a spidergram of ancient Greece, with a view to:

● preparing a talk for the class;
● making some sort of artefact to illustrate their talk;
● writing a section for a class book on 'The Greeks'.

### Organise ideas for writing

The teacher demonstrated how to research the topic of 'buildings':

● reading and browsing around the subject;
● brainstorming information to decide on categories for a spidergram;
● reading more carefully, to make notes on her spidergram.

Students followed the teacher's model to produce spidergram notes on their own topics, working in pairs. The illustration below was one pair's fourth 'draft' – as they found out more about the subject, they cut and pasted their notes, and felt increasingly confident just to use key words or pictures as 'memory-joggers' for their talk and writing.

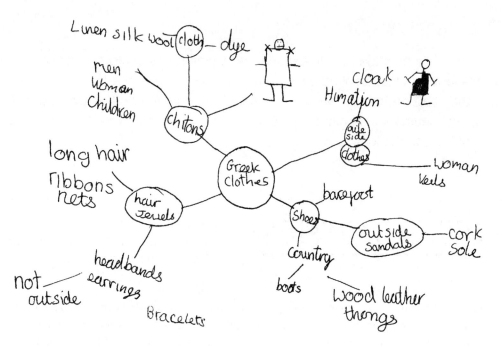

**Figure 2.2.2** Clothes spidergram

## Talk for writing

### *Read examples of the text type*

Meanwhile, the class studied samples of report text (non-fiction books from the class library), discussing the effects of:

- layout, especially headings, subheadings and captions;
- language features – the teacher especially drew their attention to impersonal and formal language constructions.

### *Talk the language of writing*

The teacher, who had modelled all aspects of the process, showed how to give a prepared talk:

- using her skeleton notes as a prompt;
- illustrating aspects of the talk with reference to the artefact she and a Special Needs pupil had created (a model of the Parthenon).

Students then gave their own talks, each member of the pair speaking alternately to cover one 'blob' of the spidergram notes.

### *Write*

The teacher demonstrated how to expand her skeleton notes into an illustrated double page spread for a class book, drawing particular attention to the layout and language features they had noticed in their earlier study. Students made their own double-page spreads, and a number of books on the Greeks were compiled, with photocopied copies for each of the contributors.

# GREEK CLOTHES

Greece is a hot country so the Ancient Greeks did not need many clothes. Also clothes were expensive and hard to keep clean.

Chitons
The main Greek clothing was called a chiton. It was like a tube of cloth pinned on top of your shoulders. Then you tied a belt round the middle. It was made of linen, silk or thin wool. Rich people dyed them in deep colours.

Men and children wore short knee length chitons. Women wore long ones because they did not work or run. In winter they might wear two chitons on top of each other.

Outside clothes
Out of the house, people wore a cloak called a himation. It went over one shoulder and under the other arm.

It was made of wool. Women put a veil over their heads and faces so men could not see them.

Hair and jewels
Greeks had long hair. Women tied it up with ribbons or a net. Inside they had silver and gold headbands and bracelets, but not outside because they might get mugged.

Shoes
People did not wear shoes inside. Outside they wore strappy sandals with cork soles.

In the countryside, rich people wore leather boots. Poor people just had bits of wood tied under their feet with leather thongs.

pins

belt

Himation

chiton

leather boots

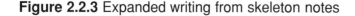

**Figure 2.2.3** Expanded writing from skeleton notes

# 2.3 Instruction case study

### Learn cross-curricular content

As part of a cross-curricular project on 'Sound', a class of ten-year-olds designed and made their own musical instruments. They worked in pairs on the understanding that, when the instruments were complete, each pair would be asked to:

- give a brief talk, explaining how to make it;
- write clear illustrated instructions for making it, aimed at younger children.

Before beginning work, the pairs were asked to discuss and draw up outline plans:

- a projected list of requirements;
- a rough diagram of the intended outcome;
- a flow-chart of the stages they intended.

They then made their instruments.

### Organise ideas for writing

These outline plans provided a starting point for skeleton notes. As they made their instruments, the students amended, annotated and added to them in another colour. This provided:

- a record of the design process;
- brief memory-joggers of all actual stages in the process, for their speaking and writing tasks. (Most pairs found it necessary to redraw the skeleton at the end, for clarity.)

## Talk for writing

### Read examples of the text type

Meanwhile, the class as a whole looked at examples of instruction text written by a previous class. They discussed the success of different sets of instructions, with particular emphasis on:

- layout and design features;
- the use of instructional language, especially imperative verbs and the way adjectives and adverbs were employed for clarity (rather than descriptive effect).

### Talk the language of writing

Pairs of students then gave their talks, using the speaking frame in the box below and their completed instruments as visual aids. The teacher spread these talks over a week, around half an hour at a time, encouraging the rest of the class to listen carefully and ask questions whenever an instruction was unclear.

## How to make...

We're going to explain how to make _____ .

*Before you start make sure you have* _____ .

You will also need  _____ .

*Begin by* _____ .

The next step is to _____ .

For further steps choose from these connectives:

*When* ____ , _____ . *After this,* ____ *Then*_____ . *Now*_____ . *While* _____ .

Finally, _____ .

*You can use your* _____ *to make a tune/rhythm like this* _____ .

### Write

Students then worked individually to expand their skeleton notes into instructions aimed at younger children. These were typed up on the computer, diagrams and illustrations scanned in, and design features added to create work-cards or booklets. A younger class tried them out, and provided feedback on their effectiveness.

How to make a shaker

You will need:

| | |
|---|---|
| a Pringles box | glitter |
| 2 handfuls of dried peas or rice | shiny coloured paper |
| a few sheets of A4 paper | scissors |
| glue | varnish |
| paint | a coloured drawing pin |

1 Make sure the inside of the Pringles box is dry. Then put in the dried peas or rice, and put the top on.
2 Put paper round to cover the Pringles box. Mark it to show where to cut, then cut it out and stick it on to cover up all the writing.
3 Place the lid on the paper and carefully draw round it. Cut out the circle and stick it on the top of the Pringles box.
4 Paint the box in a bright colour. Then leave to dry.
5 Decorate the shaker with glitter. Cut some strips of shiny paper to stick on the top. Stick them down firmly with glue and the coloured pin.
6 Varnish and leave to dry.

# 2.4 Explanation case study

### Learn cross-curricular content

As part of a science project, a class used 'physical theatre' to illustrate the way materials can change state from solid to liquid and to gas. Groups of students simulated the activity of particles in a mystery element as the teacher 'heated them up' or 'cooled them down'. When cooled down, they clustered tensely together as a solid; when warmed up, they fell to the ground and wriggled like a liquid; and warmed further, they spaced out and leapt around to simulate a gas.

### Organise ideas for writing

In pairs, students devised flowcharts to illustrate the process and explain the changes. The flowcharts were then displayed and the class discussed the most successful examples, finally producing a class flowchart.

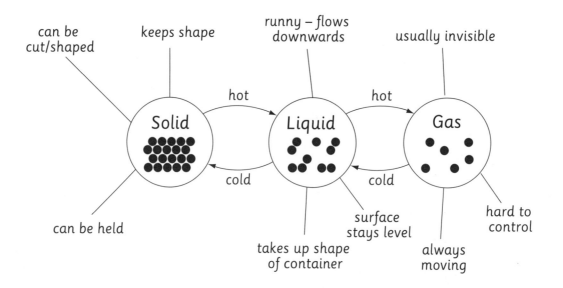

**Figure 2.4.1** Class flowchart

## Talk for writing

### Read examples of the text type

During the literacy lesson, the class looked at a familiar example of explanation – a diagram and text explaining the life cycle of a butterfly. They discussed:

- the integration of visual and verbal information;
- the characteristics of explanatory language, especially the use of technical terms and causal connectives.

### Talk the language of writing

To familiarise the class with the language of cause and effect, the teacher used an activity from *Speaking Frames: How to Teach Talk for Writing: Ages 10–14* (2011). She displayed the following 'smorgasbord' of sentence constructions:

#### Cause and effect

When ....................., _____

If ........................., _____

..........................., so_____

.................... . This causes_____

.................... . This means that_____

.................... . This results in_____

................. . As a result, _____

................. . Therefore_____

> _____ because .....................
>
> The reason _____ is that...............
>
> _____ due to ...................

(NB: Cause = ............   Effect = _____ )

She then illustrated how to use the first frame to create a silly sentence:

> **When** Mrs X eats celery, she turns into a bear.

She indicated the point where the comma separates the two chunks by drawing a large comma in the air with her finger. Students then volunteered to fill the same cause and effect into the remaining frames, indicating the comma in the same way.

> **If** Mrs X eats celery, she turns into a bear.
> Mrs X eats celery, **so** she turns into a bear.
> Mrs X eats celery. **This causes** her to turn into a bear. (Note the change in verb form.)
> Mrs X eats celery. **This means** she turns into a bear... And so on.

In pairs, they then thought up their own 'cause and effect' and took turns to fit it into the frames.

### Write

Using the class skeleton notes, students wrote their own explanation texts about solids, liquids and gases, e.g.:

*Materials are all made of tiny little bits that we cannot see, called particles. When a material is a solid, the particles are very close together so they cannot move about. This means a solid keeps its shape and you can hold it, cut it or shape it.*

*Sometimes solids (like ice, wax or iron) can be changed into liquids by heating them. Heat makes the particles more spaced out. As a result, they can move about a bit. But they are still close enough together to obey gravity, so they flow downwards. If you put liquid in a container, it flows into the shape of the container, but the top surface stays level.*

*Some liquids (e.g. water) change into gases when you heat them, because the heat makes the particles so spaced out that they don't obey gravity. This means that they move about all the time in every direction they can, and they can be very hard to control. Gases are invisible.*

*If you cool these gases down again, they will be liquids. If you cool the liquids down they go back to solids.*

# 2.5 Persuasion case study

### Learn cross-curricular content

During a project on 'Water', a class of 12-year-olds discovered how much water is used daily in the average home. They were amazed and concerned at the level of wastage, and an animated discussion ensued, at the end of which they decided to plan a publicity campaign for the rest of the school about saving water.

### Organise ideas for writing

After half an hour's research about the topic in library books or on the web, the class regrouped to pool information and organise their knowledge usage into memory-joggers in a persuasion skeleton frame.

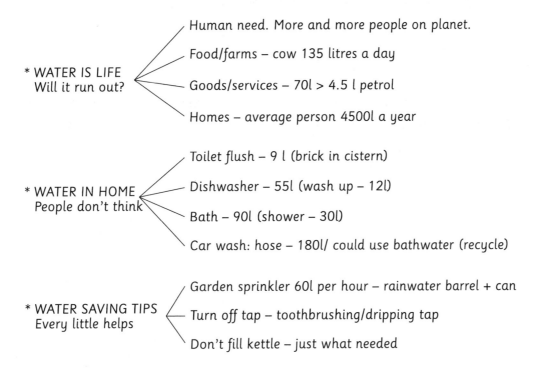

**Figure 2.5.1** Persuasion skeleton frame

## Talk for writing

### Read examples of the text type

It was agreed that the publicity campaign should include leaflets, posters and a presentation to the rest of the school. The class therefore collected examples of each type of persuasion text, including looking at a DVD of famous political party broadcasts. They looked particularly at:

- the importance of arguing a case;
- the layout and design of posters and leaflets;
- the language of persuasion.

### Talk the language of writing

Students used their skeleton notes as the basis of a presentation to be given in assembly. They worked in three groups, each group taking one bullet point from the persuasion skeleton and devising the best way to:

- convey the main point;
- back it up with argument/evidence;
- win the hearts and minds of the audience.

Two students worked out speeches to introduce and link the sections, and the 'Water Is Life' presentation was delivered as part of a school assembly.

### Write

Pairs of children then used the skeleton notes to produce posters and leaflets backing up the assembly message. They duplicated copies for other classes to display/read.

# 2.6 Discussion case study

### Learn cross-curricular content

During a visit to a local art gallery, some 13-year-old pupils expressed their dislike of the non-representational paintings, while others appreciated them. The teacher brought a postcard of one particularly disputed painting into school, and enlarged on a 'visualiser' so all the class could see and discuss it.

### Organise ideas for writing

After time for paired talk, the class compiled notes on both sides of the argument on a discussion skeleton framework.

## Is *Bojewan Farms* a good painting?

| AGAINST | FOR |
| --- | --- |
| Doesn't look like farm | Painting/not photograph |
| Mix-up colours/shapes | Atmosphere/feelings |
| Should look like real place | |
| | |
| Colours – boring, sludgy, ugly | Looks like the land/weather |
| | Hard work/strength in farming |
| | Spots of blue, red, gold, white – like sea, flowers, corn, snow |
| | |
| Confusing. Mixed up | Impressions – not pictures |
| Not finished off – baby | Animals/machinery/people |
| could've done it | Baby couldn't do that |
| | |
| Doesn't make you | Can look for ages – see different things |
| want to stop and look | at different times |
| | Different people see it different ways |

## Talk for writing

### Read examples of the text type and talk the language of writing

In the literacy lesson, the teacher provided a speaking frame from *Speaking Frames: How to Teach Talk for Writing: Ages 10–14,* and asked pupils in groups of six to compile arguments on both sides of a controversial question. Each group had a different topic – homework, school uniform, fox-hunting, assessment on coursework instead of tests, shortening the school lunch break. The groups then fed back their findings using the frame, with each group member completing one box in the frame.

There is a great deal of debate about whether_____ .

*Some people believe that_____ .*
*They argue that_____ .*

However, other people claim that_____ .

*Another argument often put in favour of_____ is that_____ .*

On the other hand, it could be said that_____ .

*Supporters of_____ point out that_____ , while opponents reply*
*that_____ .*

On the whole, we think we agree with supporters/critics that_____ .

### Write

Students were then asked to write a script for a short local radio broadcast about Peter Lanyon's painting *Bojewans Farms*.

# PART 3

# Teaching materials

## Using the teaching materials

Learning to write is a long, slow process. The teaching materials provided here are designed to be used at different stages in that process, for different purposes (but please don't use each one more than once, or your students will quite rightly rebel, or die of boredom – the basic principles can be applied to texts found across the curriculum).

For each text type you will find:

- basic information on the text type (in the case of **recount** and **report,** which are the most frequently used in cross-curricular work, information is provided for two key variations);
- photocopiable sample text(s);
- analysis of each sample's structure and major language features;
- four pages of suggestions for teaching writing, illustrating possible progression in terms of learning objectives between ages 8 and 14.

## Shared, Guided and Independent Writing

The major teaching model adopted is that of Shared, Guided and Independent Writing. As shown in the diagram below, this allows for varying levels of support, depending on students' experience and writing competence.

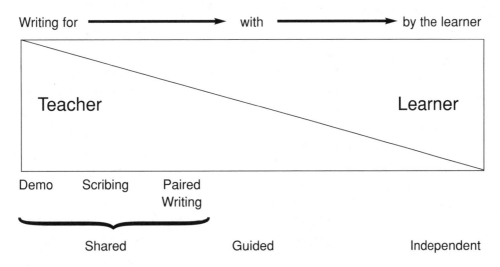

**Figure 3.1** Varying levels of support

It takes many years to build up the knowledge and skills covered in this book. Each time a particular text type is used for cross-curricular writing, there's an opportunity to revise previous teaching and to focus on a new aspect of writing. This will probably require a high level of teaching input (**Shared Writing** – see below). Students then need time and opportunities to apply what they've revised and learned in real meaningful writing tasks: i.e. **Independent Writing**.

Some students, of course, require more support than others during Independent Writing. This support may be provided in a variety of ways, e.g.:

- let two students support each other in Paired Writing (see 'Successful Paired Writing', below);
- work with them in a Guided Writing group (see 'Guided Writing' below);
- ask the students to imitate what they've just seen you do, by composing their own versions of the piece you've demonstrated in Shared Writing;
- provide a limited or staged version of the writing task (e.g. 'Just write the introductory paragraph, then come and check with me');
- provide some sort of support materials, to 'scaffold out' certain areas of difficulty, e.g. vocabulary/spelling list, sentence starts, a 'cloze' version of the task.

## Shared Writing

When introducing or re-introducing a text type, it's always worthwhile starting with Shared Writing. This involves a mixture of techniques, as appropriate to your teaching aims and the dynamics of your classroom on the day.

**Table 3.1** Techniques for Shared Writing

| Demonstration | Scribing | Paired Writing |
|---|---|---|
| Model the process of writing for the students. | Use scribing to pull the class in, especially if they're beginning to shuffle, or if there's an opportunity to follow up some sentence level teaching. | Every so often, ask pairs of students to work on a section of text together. This could be oral composition or a short written piece. |
| Write a section of text on the board or flipchart, and provide a commentary on what you are doing and why. | | |
| Demonstrate exactly how the ideas get out of your head and onto the page. | Invite the class to contribute ideas, forms of words, alternative constructions, etc. | Ensure they understand the content and the language features concerned. The most effective tasks involve students putting something you've just taught into immediate practice. |
| It is almost impossible to compose and commentate at the same time. You need a script – work it out beforehand. | Choose the most successful and integrate them into the demonstration, still keeping up the commentary. | Give a time limit, then ask for feedback – and proceed as for scribing. |

You can use our text analysis pages to plan a script and commentary, selecting grammatical concepts appropriate to the age group.

### Integrating Shared Writing lessons with cross-curricular work

If it's something specific, like 'how to write an introductory paragraph', demonstrate on a piece of writing based on current cross-curricular learning (e.g. *The Battle of Salamis*). If appropriate, ask students to finish the account during Independent Writing.

You can use a skeleton here to save time. Give one paragraph/ section to each pair/group of students and ask them to take responsibility for writing it up. Make a composite piece from the best submissions. In a subsequent lesson, discuss and edit to improve content and coherence.

At a later date give students the chance to try out what they've learned from your demonstration on another similar piece of writing (e.g. *The Battle of Marathon*): this time they could complete the whole piece.

If it's a more general objective, such as the use of organisational devices, choose one section for Shared Writing (make sure it's not always the opening paragraph) and ask students to write the rest.

You could divide this task up between pairs/groups or let each student complete the whole piece.

---

## Successful Paired Writing

- Choose the best way to pair students for your teaching style and class. Some teachers allocate 'writing partners' (and revise them if they don't work), based on students who have something to offer each other (e.g. a bright dyslexic and a competent plodder). Others work on an ad hoc basis, expecting students to work with whoever they happen to sit next to.
- Spend time training the class into this routine:

| | |
|---|---|
| Rehearse | Work out what you're going to write orally first. Listen to how it sounds, and improve it if you can. |
| Write | Either one writes while the other helps, or both write their own version (the latter can save squabbles). This is another opportunity to edit as you go. |
| Read | Read the whole of the shared piece aloud. Again, edit if necessary. |

- Give a time limit for short bursts of Paired Writing and emphasise the urgency of the task. You can adjust the time limit if necessary, but you don't want students thinking there's time to waste.

## Guided Writing

While the whole class is engaged in Independent Writing, the teacher is free to home in on the needs of a specific group of students. This is an opportunity to provide focused help with those areas of word, sentence or text level work of particular significance. You may choose to work with an ability group, or you may create an ad hoc group of students that you've noticed need help on one aspect of writing. In either case, the overall writing task provides a context for focused teaching.

## Planning and plenary

The words planning and plenary are linked by more than alliteration. A 'plenary session' at the end of a lesson is a chance to revise its main points which, of course, means returning to your initial teaching objectives.

This book is intended to serve as an overall planning device:

- Use the 'two horses' model on page 1 to link non-fiction writing to work across the curriculum. Possible links are suggested on pages 5–8.
- Select specific literacy teaching objectives from the year-by-year teaching pages of the text units.
- Display your main objective(s) for each lesson so students are aware of the point of the lesson.

Teaching is a messy business, and no one can ever plan the exact course of a lesson. Don't try to stick rigidly to a plan if it doesn't seem to be working – and don't assume that, just because you've 'covered' some objectives, the students have automatically learned them.

It is, however, always useful to *review the main points* you're trying to get over at regular intervals, and at the end of a particular course of teaching. This sort of plenary review is likely to be even more useful if the students are directly involved, and given the chance to *articulate what they have learned.*

- At the very least, take a few minutes to remind students of the main points you have covered. Make this review as interactive as possible, e.g.:
  - Go through the displayed objectives and ask students whether you can tick each one off.
  - Ask students to suggest what are today's 'key words', and list the best answers on the board (plus any important ones they miss).
  - Use an aide-memoire, such as the Text structure and Language features lists on pages, 38, 50, 62, 70, 78 and 80.
  - Use the text you have produced during 'Shared Writing' to remind students of the key points by highlighting/annotating.
- At the end of a sequence of lessons, you may make over a whole lesson to plenary review. Provide opportunities for students to articulate what they have learned, e.g.:
  - Use one of the speaking and listening activities (10–11) as a means of reviewing what has been learned.
  - Ask pupils in groups to discuss the text type you have just covered and come up with their own list of key writing points.

   – Give pairs of students a text type checklist (see Stage 4 of each text unit) and a published example of the text type to pick holes in.

## Purpose + audience → form and style

This equation sums up the process of planning a piece of non-fiction writing. The experienced writer assesses each element almost instantaneously, but students need time to think and consider, so that the process will become similarly automatic for them.

Take time to discuss the four key questions:

1  What is the purpose of this particular piece of non-fiction?
2  For whom is it intended (and what do we know about them)?
3  How will these two facts affect the form of the writing?
4  How will they affect the style you choose to write in?

### Purpose

The general purpose will determine the text type and structure, depending on whether you want to:

- retell events → recount;
- describe the characteristics of something → report;
- tell someone how to do or make something → instruction;
- explain how or why something happens → explanation;
- persuade someone to agree with your point of view → persuasion;
- present a balanced argument → discussion.

But each individual piece of writing will also have a more specific purpose. The purpose of each of our sample pieces is given on the analysis page. Encourage students to think clearly about the specific purpose of any writing they are intending, and to consider how it will affect the form.

### Audience

The form and style of a piece of writing vary considerably depending on the audience, e.g. is the audience:

- yourself → you know exactly how much detail is required, and can dispense with formalities;
- a personal friend or friends → you have a good idea how much background detail is necessary, and can write informally;
- a person/people you don't know personally, but whom you know something about (e.g. age, interests, the level of background knowledge they are likely to have) → you can probably gauge how much background information is necessary, and how explicit you have to be, but your style will be reasonably formal;
- a remote and unknown audience → writing must be explicit and probably formal.

Encourage students always to consider the exact audience for whom they are about to write, and to think how it will affect their approach and style.

## *Form*

There are a number of obvious forms writing can take depending upon purpose. As part of their writing across the curriculum, you will probably want pupils to produce books (or sections of books), booklets, essays and various other kinds of text, such as:

- **personal communication**: letters, notes, messages, blogs;
- **journalistic writing**: newspaper reports, editorials, obituaries;
- **note-taking and making**: lists, notes, charts and other formats;
- **publicity material**: posters, jingles, leaflets, pamphlets;
- **formal documents**: CV, police report, school report.

On the first page of each Text Unit, we list a selection of forms of writing which are typical of the text type. There is guidance on some major conventions in Appendix 1, but since conventions are best established by discussion of a variety of sample texts, it is helpful to build up your own portfolio.

Another aspect of form is presentation. Students need to consider layout and organisation of material on the page, and to select appropriately from the wide range of presentational devices available to them, including headings and sub-headings, bullet points, numbering, use of diagrams and other graphic organisers, boxes and various attention-grabbing devices. All of these are covered within the text unit teaching pages.

## *Style*

To some extent, style must be a personal thing – even in non-fiction writing, we want to encourage students to find their own 'voice' and to make decisions about approach and tone. But many elements of style are determined by purpose, audience and form. For instance, every piece of writing must find a place somewhere along the following continua:

| | |
|---|---|
| subjective ——————————————————— | objective |
| personal ——————————————————— | impersonal |
| informal ——————————————————— | formal |

The position on each continuum has an effect on vocabulary, sentence construction and other grammatical elements, as is illustrated in the analysis of language features in each text unit. Students should be aware of the significance of these factors, and able to adjust their own use of language as appropriate.

# 3.1 Recount text

## Personal recounts

**Purpose**: To retell events (from the point of view of someone who was there).
**Example**: First person account of a school trip, written like a 'news' piece.

### Text structure

- orientation: setting the scene – who, what, where, when?;
- sequential organisation – what happened, in time order;
- closing statement(s) – bringing the writing to a satisfactory conclusion;
- basic skeleton framework – a **timeline** ('this happened, then this happened, etc.').

### Language features

- past tense (specific events that only happened once);
- time connectives and other devices to aid chronological structure;
- first person writing;
- focus on specific participants, including writer.

## Key teaching points

- Personal recount text is one of the easiest types of non-fiction writing, since first-person narrative comes naturally to human beings. We all tell stories about our lives, and there is probably a need to tidy memory into a neat narrative form.
- However, personal recount covers a range of different types of text, from the informal, subjective writing in personal diaries and letters, to the formal, objective writing up of a science experiment. The issue of **purpose** and **audience** is often particularly significant in the writing of personal recounts.
- Many students also need help in organising information into **chronological order**. If facts or experiences are new to them, they often omit or confuse events. Preliminary organisation on a time-line can help students recall information and see its place in the overall sequence of events.
- The completed timeline may also be used as a paragraph planner. Before writing, students can draw lines across the timeline to designate appropriate paragraph breaks.

Common forms of **personal recount text**:

- letter;
- autobiography;
- diary or journal;
- newspaper report;
- magazine article;
- write-up of a trip or activity;
- account of science experiment.

# A trip to the Eden Project

Last Friday, our class travelled in the school bus to visit the Eden Project in Cornwall. It was a long ride to get there so we had to be at school an hour early, at eight o'clock. We brought our breakfast to eat on the bus.

When we arrived at the Eden Project, we could tell it was a big attraction by the size of the car parks which were carefully laid out and named after fruits – we were in Plum Car Park. As we walked down, we could see the Eden Project buildings – two enormous plastic domes, built in a dip in the ground.

Mrs Jeffries told us they were called 'biomes' and the dip used to be a claypit, where men had dug out the clay to use for making pots. We spent our morning going round the biomes, looking at the plants. One is kept very warm inside and filled with tropical plants like rubber trees, bamboo, spices, coconuts and pineapples. There are also displays of buildings and gardens from tropical countries. The other biome is not so warm and among the plants there are oranges, lemons, grapes and olives.

We had our lunch in the exhibition centre, where we watched a video about 'The Making of Eden'. The Eden Project was built to show how men and plants depend upon each other, and it cost millions of pounds to build. Next we had a talk about the plants. A lady explained how you get cocoa beans and cocoa milk from a pod, and use them to make chocolate.

We were allowed to look in the shop, and spend two pounds. I bought some stickers and a postcard of a man building the biomes. Finally, it was time for the long ride home. We were back by half past three, just in time for the bell.

<table>
<tr><td>

**Purpose**

1  To recount the events of a significant day (a school trip).

2  To provide objective factual information about the Eden Project.

</td><td>

**+**

</td><td>

**Audience**

Readers who know the writer (or at least are familiar with his/her background, or perhaps the writer him/herself.

</td></tr>
</table>

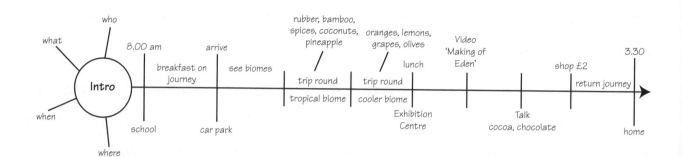

## Organisation and content

***Title:*** straightforward summary of content to follow.

### Introduction

**Paragraph 1:** Provides details of
  *who* (our class)
  *what* (trip to Eden Project)
  *when* (last Friday, setting off early)
  *where* (in Cornwall).

### Recount

The outward journey is dealt with in paragraph 1.

**Paragraph 2:** arrival at the Eden Project and first impressions.

**Paragraph 3:** the tour of the biomes (including information on the building of the Eden Project).

**Paragraph 4:** lunch and the afternoon's events (including information on the purpose of the Eden Project).

### Conclusion

**Final paragraph:** the end of the trip, return journey and arrival home.

### A trip to the Eden Project

Last Friday, our class travelled in the school bus to visit the Eden Project in Cornwall. It was a long ride to get there so we had to be at school an hour early, at eight o'clock. We brought our breakfast to eat on the bus.

When we arrived at the Eden Project, we could tell it was a big attraction by the size of the car parks which were carefully laid out and named after fruits – we were in Plum Car Park. As we walked down, we could see the Eden Project buildings – two enormous plastic domes, built in a dip in the ground.

Mrs Jeffries told us they were called 'biomes' and the dip used to be a claypit, where men had dug out the clay to use for making pots. We spent our morning going round the biomes, looking at the plants. One is kept very warm inside and filled with tropical plants like rubber trees, bamboo, spices, coconuts and pineapples. There are also displays of buildings and gardens from tropical countries. The other biome is not so warm and among the plants there are oranges, lemons, grapes and olives.

We had our lunch in the exhibition centre, where we watched a video about 'The Making of Eden'. The Eden Project was built to show how men and plants depend upon each other, and it cost millions of pounds to build. Next we had a talk about the plants. A lady explained how you get cocoa beans and cocoa milk from a pod, and use them to make chocolate.

We were allowed to look in the shop, and spend two pounds. I bought some stickers and a postcard of a man building the biomes. Finally, it was time for the long ride home. We were back by half past three, just in time for the bell.

**Form and style**

- Personal recount text – an account in diary format.
- Events in chronological order.

- Significant detail, including examples, as personally recalled.
- Objective, factual description.

## Language features

### Specific language

- Mostly written in the **past tense**, because the trip was a specific event, which only happened once. However, the third paragraph, describing the project, is in the **present tense** because the information is general: the things described continue to exist once the trip is over.
- **Specific participants** – 'our class'.

### Personal language

- Written in the **first person** (mostly plural: *our class, we* but with a singular reference in the final paragraph: *I*).
- The writer assumes a high level of background knowledge on behalf of the reader: references to *last Friday, our class, school, Mrs Jeffries.*
- Despite the personal language, however, this is a highly objective account (see below).

### Time and sequence

- Exact timings for the **beginning** and **end** of the excursion help establish that time is an important element in this chronological account: *Last Friday... at school an hour early, at eight o'clock; half past three, just in time for the bell.*

- **Paragraphing** helps clarify timing: each paragraph deals with a well-defined section of the day (see 'Organisation', opposite).
- **Sequential connectives** to open sentences (*When...As...Next...Finally...*) help to indicate the sequence of events.

### Informative language

While the account is a personal one, it is objective rather than subjective. The author recounts what happened on the trip, but makes no personal comments or value judgements. There is no attempt to engage or excite the reader.

- Basic **verbs** (*went, get, brought, arrived, walked,* etc.).
- Descriptive language (**adjectives** and **adverbs**) provide factual detail, rather than effect (*a long bus ride, a big attraction, enormous domes, very warm, not so warm*).
- Description sometimes based on logical **deduction** (*we could tell it was a big attraction by the size of the car parks*).
- Provision of **examples** (*tropical plants like... among the plants there are...*).
- Emphasis on **sources of information/ evidence**: *Mrs Jeffries told us...we could see...we watched a video...we had a talk...a lady explained how...*

## Impersonal recounts

**Purpose**: To retell events (from an impersonal standpoint).
**Example**: Third person account of a school outing, written as a magazine article.

### Text structure

- orientation: setting the scene — who, what, where, when?;
- sequential organisation – what happened, in time order;
- closing statement(s) – bringing the writing to a satisfactory conclusion;
- basic skeleton framework – a **timeline** ('this happened, then this happened, etc.').

### Language features

- past tense (specific events that only happened once);
- time connectives and other devices to aid chronological structure;
- third person writing;
- focus on specific participants (named individuals/groups).

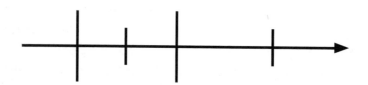

## Key teaching points

- Impersonal recount text clearly shares many characteristics with **narrative** writing, and is therefore sometimes considered one of the easiest types of non-fiction writing.
- However, impersonal recount covers a range of different types of writing, from informal, subjective, value-laden accounts in magazines, to the formal, objective writing of a scientific report. The issue of **purpose** and **audience** is often particularly significant in the writing of impersonal recounts.
- Many students also need considerable help in organising information into **chronological order**. Preliminary organisation of the information on a timeline can help students recall information and see its place in the overall sequence of events.

- The completed timeline may also be used as a paragraph planner. Before writing, students can draw lines across the timeline to designate appropriate paragraph breaks.

---

Common forms of **impersonal recount text**:

- non-fiction book (e.g. history);
- biography;
- magazine article;
- newspaper report;
- encyclopaedia entry;
- obituary;
- account of science experiment.

---

# A taste of paradise

'All this way to see plants in a greenhouse!' After two hours watching rain stream by the bus windows on the long road to Cornwall last Friday, Year 8 was feeling less than enthusiastic about visiting the Eden Project. Yet as the students made their way across the vast car-parks, catching their first glimpse of two huge plastic 'biomes' in a gigantic crater, they began to change their minds.

The Eden Project is the largest greenhouse in the world, big enough to hold the Tower of London, and housing more than 135,000 plants. In the humid tropical biome, Year 8 found themselves wandering through a South American rain forest, basking in a Polynesian garden, sighing in the stifling heat beside a tropical waterfall. They saw plants they knew – bananas, pineapples, mangoes, cocoa, rice – not picked and packaged on supermarket shelves, but alive and growing. They saw plants they didn't know, and hadn't dreamed of. They began to realise how much human beings depend on nature for all their basic needs – food, drink, shelter, clothing – and luxuries – sweets, cosmetics, sportsgear...

In the warm temperate biome, the heat was gentler, and the air filled with the scent of lemons. Here they saw the plants of California and the Mediterranean: olives, vines, tobacco, cotton, cork, and mouthwatering fruit and vegetables. Outside, on the slopes leading up to the exhibition hall, were the familiar plants of the cool temperate zone, and the familiar weather – still raining!

After lunch, there was a film about the building of Eden and a talk from the education department... and then the long drive home. But now as the rain beat down and the windows steamed up, Year 8 could close their eyes and remember Paradise. The scents of jasmine, ginger and pineapple; the sultry tropical heat; the rainbow colours of wild, exotic flowers. Some plants; some greenhouse!

| Purpose | | Audience |
|---|---|---|
| 1  To recount the events of a significant day (a school trip).<br><br>2  To provide factual information about the Eden Project.<br><br>3  To engage and entertain the reader. |  | Readers of a school magazine or newspaper (students, parents, governors — many of them unknown to the writer). |

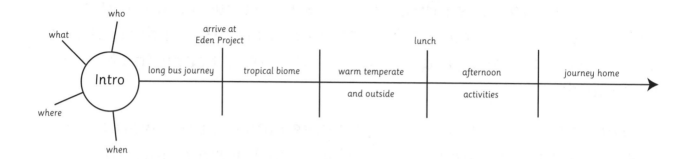

## Organisation and content

***Title:*** Eye-catching title to attract attention: quote from *Bounty* advert; play on words (Eden/Paradise).

### Introduction

**Paragraph 1:** Provides details of
>   *who* (our class)
>   *what* (trip to Eden Project)
>   *when* (last Friday)
>   *where* (in Cornwall)

Establishes atmosphere of a rainy coach ride, negative feelings (especially negative opening line). On arrival at Eden Project, change of tone – positive.

### Events in chronological order

The outward journey and arrival at the Eden Project is dealt with in paragraph 1.

**Paragraph 2:** Upbeat: factual information re Eden Project. Evocative description of trip round tropical biome. Final sentence sums up Eden Project's message (interdependence of humans and plants).

**Paragraph 3:** Evocative description of trip round warm temperate biome. Brief description of outside zone – 'still raining' contrasts with the lushness of the biomes.

### Conclusion

**Paragraph 4:** Summary of the afternoon's events. Return journey – returns to theme of wet coach ride, but with positive slant. Final line is a riposte to the negative opening.

---

### A taste of paradise

'All this way to see plants in a greenhouse!' After two hours watching rain stream by the bus windows on the long road to Cornwall last Friday, Year 8 was feeling less than enthusiastic about visiting the Eden Project. Yet as the students made their way across the vast car-parks, catching their first glimpse of two huge plastic 'biomes' in a gigantic crater, they began to change their minds.

The Eden Project is the largest greenhouse in the world, big enough to hold the Tower of London, and housing more than 135,000 plants. In the humid tropical biome, Year 8 found themselves wandering through a South American rain forest, basking in a Polynesian garden, sighing in the stifling heat beside a tropical waterfall. They saw plants they knew – bananas, pineapples, mangoes, cocoa, rice – not picked and packaged on supermarket shelves, but alive and growing. They saw plants they didn't know, and hadn't dreamed of. They began to realise how much human beings depend on nature for all their basic needs – food, drink, shelter, clothing – and luxuries – sweets, cosmetics, sportsgear...

In the warm temperate biome, the heat was gentler, and the air filled with the scent of lemons. Here they saw the plants of California and the Mediterranean: olives, vines, tobacco, cotton, cork, and mouthwatering fruit and vegetables. Outside, on the slopes leading up to the exhibition hall, were the familiar plants of the cool temperate zone, and the familiar weather – still raining!

After lunch, there was a film about the building of Eden and a talk from the education department... and then the long drive home. But now as the rain beat down and the windows steamed up, Year 8 could close their eyes and remember Paradise. The scents of jasmine, ginger and pineapple; the sultry tropical heat; the rainbow colours of wild, exotic flowers. Some plants; some greenhouse!

## Form and style

- Third-person recount text – a magazine feature.
- Events in chronological order.

- Significant detail, including examples.
- Descriptive, engaging writing style.

## Language features

### *Specific language*

- Mostly written in the **past tense**, because the trip was a specific event, which only happened once. However, the opening of paragraph 2, describing the project, is in the **present tense** because the information is general: the things described continue to exist once the trip is over.
- **Specific participants** – 'Year 8'.

### *Impersonal language*

- Written in the **third person** (mostly plural: *Year 8, the students*). We do not know who the author is – could be a member of Year 8, the teacher, an accompanying reporter...
- Despite the impersonal stance, however, this is a highly subjective account (see below).

### *Time and sequence*

- **Paragraphing** helps clarify timing: each paragraph deals with a well-defined section of the day (see 'Organisation', opposite).
- **Sequential connectives** to open sentences (*After two hours...After lunch...*) help to indicate the sequence of events, but most of the chronology is carried in the layout.

### *Use of language to engage and entertain*

While this recount provides much the same information as 'Recount 1', the use of language is much more subjective – it has been carefully chosen to engage the reader, and to persuade him/her of the attractions of the Eden Project (see also 'Persuasion text').

- **Direct speech** for opening line draws reader in.
- Descriptive language including **powerful verbs** (*wandering, basking, sighing* etc.) and **adjectives** (*stifling, mouthwatering, sultry, tropical, wild, exotic*).
- Frequent use of **lists**, to suggest lushness and plenty, e.g. lists of plants, plant uses, memories through different senses on the trip home.
- Use of **repetition** for effect: (*They saw plants they knew... They saw plants they didn't know; familiar plants...familiar weather*).
- **Alliteration** (*picked and packaged; jasmine, ginger...*).
- Use of **contrast**: the rainy journey contrasted with the tropical heat; the **students'** negative feelings on the way, contrasted with their changed outlook on the way back.
- **Variety of sentence construction**. In paragraph 2, a repeated sentence construction (*They saw...They saw...They began to realise...*) creates a cumulative effect. In paragraph 3, sentences open with adverbials of place (*In the warm temperate biome...Here... Outside...*).
- Use of **connectives** to create contrast: in both the first and final paragraph the key effect is a contrast (negative rainy journey/positive Eden project). Both these hinge on a connective: paragraph 1 *Yet...* paragraph 4 *But...* The tone of the writing on either side of the connective is very different.

## Recount writing: stage 1

### Content and organisation

Focus on chronological order.

Help students recognise how events are sequenced and how they can be represented in skeleton form by:

- converting the information in a recount text into brief notes on a timeline (see examples on pages 40 and 44);
- creating timelines for events studied in history or other subjects;
- creating timeline records of school events, such as outings.

### Language features

- Verbs and tense – stress past tense by using it on timeline notes. (This doesn't come naturally – it's more obvious to write notes in present tense, which leads some students to wander into the present when writing their recounts.)
- Powerful verbs, adjectives – these are important features of vivid recount writing.
- Demonstrate how to select appropriate ones during Shared Writing.
- Sequential connectives – collect examples from reading and display on a poster.
- First and third person – illustrate with the sample recounts or other suitable texts.

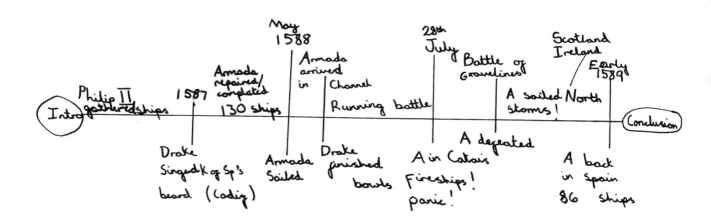

### Making timelines

- Make a rough timeline first (this can be a useful way of familiarising yourself with the information to be taught, and may be used as lesson notes).
- Create timelines for class use in a variety of ways, e.g.:
  - a large timeline on a roll of wallpaper;
  - a human timeline – write events on cards and give to students to organise themselves in appropriate order;
  - a washing timeline – write events on card and peg along a washing line.
- Don't worry about exact time markings: just generally link length of time to distance along line.
- Use vertical lines to note specific events; write ongoing events along the line.

## Recount writing: stage 2

### *Content and organisation*

Continue to focus on chronological order (as Stage 1).

- As a note-taking activity, ask students to create brief timeline notes of familiar events such as the school day, what they did at the weekend or during a holiday.
- Occasionally ask a student to make notes on a class activity, e.g. when someone is unable to take part in gym or games, ask him/her to take notes of the main events of the lesson and use them to create a timeline.
- As a class, take brief notes on the content of a television programme and arrange as a timeline.
- Any of these timeline skeletons may be used as the basis of a piece of recount writing.

### *Language features*

- Powerful verbs, adjectives, adverbs – these are important for engaging and entertaining your audience when writing newspaper-type reports. Compare the effectiveness of our examples:
  - example 1 (p. 30) basic verbs, factual adjectives;
  - example 2 (p. 43) powerful verbs, vivid adjectives.
- Word order – this can be covered when working on writing an introductory paragraph (see below). Concentrate on the first four questions in the box. Demonstrate how to summarise the key facts in a couple of sentences, by making very brief notes in response to each question. Show how these facts can be linked together and turned into complete sentences. Encourage students to try a variety of different ways of crafting the opening sentences – use a mixture of oral work, scribing and Paired Writing (see pages 32–4).

### Writing an introductory paragraph

Newspaper reports should always answer these key questions in their opening paragraph:

> *who* is it about?
> *what* happened?
> *when* did it happen?
> *where* did it happen?
> *why* should my reader bother to find out more?

The first four questions provide basic background information which orientates the reader, and makes the subsequent text easier to follow.

The final question is about 'hooking' the reader's attention.

This is actually a good formula for the opening paragraph of any recount piece.

## Recount writing: stage 3

### Content and organisation

Focus on paragraphing:

- In reading recounts, note how the author has decided on paragraph breaks, e.g. in our first example, ask students to summarise the content of each paragraph.
- Continue work on chronological order (see Stages 1 and 2). Expect pupils to create timeline notes for themselves in history and other subjects.
- Use timeline notes from other curricular areas as the basis for recount writing. Before writing, discuss the best way to divide the information on the timeline into paragraphs.
- Draw vertical coloured lines through the timeline to show where the paragraph breaks will come. Use these as a guide when writing.

### Language features

- Writing for different audiences and purposes:
  - Personal versus impersonal writing: illustrate the difference with our examples or other suitable texts. Look for further examples. Discuss which might be more appropriate for various audiences, e.g. young children, university experts, magazine readers, people looking up information in an encyclopaedia.
  - Subjective versus objective writing: illustrate with our examples or other suitable texts and look for further examples. Discuss which might be more appropriate for various audiences, as above.
- Reported and direct speech:
  - Reported speech can be quicker and can gloss over details e.g. in Recount 1, *Mrs Jeffries told us that . . . A lady explained how . . .* Investigate the construction, tense (always past) and person (third). Try changing to direct speech.
  - Direct speech (a direct quotation) can be used in non-fiction writing for effect – it's more immediately impactful and vivid, e.g. opening line of Recount 2.

### Reordering sentences

Choose suitable sentences from recount text to cut up into chunks and write on cards. Students should hold these to make a human sentence, or you can peg them on a washing line. Try reorganising them in various ways to see if (a) it alters the meaning (b) you can improve the rhythm or emphasis. For instance in Recount 1, try:

- *Last Friday / our class / travelled / in the school bus / to visit the Eden Project / in Cornwall.*
- *As we walked down / we could see / the Eden Project buildings / two enormous plastic domes / built in a dip in the ground.*

On the whole, you'll find it's adverbial chunks (answering the questions *when*, *where* and *how*) that can be moved around most easily. The choice of chunk with which you open the sentence affects the emphasis. Word order also has an effect on punctuation.

## Recount writing: stage 4

### Content and organisation

- Create blank timelines ('zigzag books' made of several sheets of paper stuck together) divided into equal sections (one for each year of your students' lives). Ask students to make autobiographical timelines for homework. Suggest they illustrate these with photographs and other documentation.
- On the basis of the timeline, ask students to design an autobiographical booklet, with a number of short chapters, in which the photos, etc. can be interpolated as the text is written.
- When studying famous people in history, R.E., etc., make biographical timelines. Divide into paragraphs (see page 46) and use as the basis for biographical writing.

### Language features

- Introductory paragraph: revise Stage 2 concepts, adding that in biographical writing, the opening should also sum up, or give a clue to, the reason the subject was famous.
- Connecting words and phrases; complex sentences: collect examples of effective words, phrases and sentence constructions from reading of biographies and display on a wall poster for pupils to use when they are writing.

## Recount checklist

### Organisation

- Does the introductory paragraph answer the questions *who, what, where, when* so that the reader has a rough idea of what the piece will be about?  ☐
- Does the introductory paragraph also draw the reader in by suggesting *why* the topic is worth reading about (or, in the case of biography, why the subject became famous)?  ☐
- Is the recount in clear chronological order?  ☐
- Is this supported by the positioning of paragraph breaks?  ☐
- Is there a closing statement, bringing the timeline to a satisfactory conclusion?  ☐

### Language features

- Is the text consistently in the past tense (except for references to places/circumstances which are ongoing)?  ☐
- Is the text consistently in the first person or third person, depending on whether it is a personal or impersonal recount?  ☐
- Does the text use vocabulary and sentence structures appropriate to the audience?  ☐
- Are there time connectives and other devices to aid the chronological structure?  ☐

# 3.2 Report text

## Non-comparative reports

**Purpose**: to describe the characteristics of something.
**Example**: an extract from a general encyclopaedia.

### Text structure

- introductory information about what is to be described: who, what, when, where (overall classification);
- non-chronological organisation;
- description organised according to categories of information;
- basic skeleton framework – a **spidergram** (one spider leg per category; which could divide into further spider legs, depending on degree of detail).

### Language features

- present tense (except historical reports);
- usually general nouns and pronouns (not particular people or things);
- third person writing;
- factual writing, often involving technical words and phrases.

## Key teaching points

- Non-comparative report text deals with a single topic, which may be wide-ranging, e.g. *Ancient Greece* or *Birds*, or more focused, e.g. *The Scottish Wildcat.*
- The difference between report and recount is that report text is usually non-chronological (although there are occasional reports which can be chronologically organised, e.g. a generalised *Day in the Life of...* which is not about a specific day or person). The basic skeletons for the two text types show this difference clearly.
- Learning to organise report text involves categorising information. This is a natural human thinking strategy, but since most early written accounts are chronological, many apprentice writers find it difficult to adapt to a non-chronological approach. The making of spidergram skeletons is helpful in re-orientating their attitude to the information.
- There are three stages in making a spidergram (see learning to BOS, page 59), which provide an opportunity to think holistically about the subject matter before committing ideas to writing. This exercise is valuable for all writers, whatever their level of linguistic competence.
- There are other ways of representing report text (e.g. a picture, labelled diagram, plan or map) which may be used instead of or in addition to the spidergram.

---

Common forms of **non-comparative report text**:

- information leaflet;
- school project file;
- tourist guide book;
- encyclopaedia entry;
- magazine article;
- non-fiction book (e.g. geography);
- letter.

# Butterflies

Butterflies belong to the order of insects known as Lepidoptera. This means they have scaly bodies and wings, and a feeding tube on the front of the head, called a proboscis, coiled up when not in use. Their wings may be large, brightly coloured and patterned. Butterflies are found in most parts of the world, and different species are adapted to the environments in which they live.

Like all insects, the butterfly's body is divided into three parts: head, thorax and abdomen. On the head are a pair of antennae, used for smelling, and two large compound eyes. Three pairs of legs and two pairs of wings – fore and hind – grow from the thorax. The wings are made of a very thin membrane, stretched over a framework of 'veins', in the same way as the skin of an umbrella is stretched over the frame. Tiny overlapping scales on the membrane give the wings their pattern and colour.

Male butterflies tend to be more brightly coloured than the females, but the females are larger. They also have bigger wings, enabling them to fly even when they are carrying a heavy burden of eggs. A female butterfly may lay up to 3,000 eggs, always choosing the appropriate plant for the caterpillars to feed on. However, usually only one or two eggs out of a hundred hatch out and many others die as they grow through the stages of larva (caterpillar) and chrysalis (pupa) to become an imago (adult butterfly).

The imago usually has a life span of only a few weeks. It feeds on nectar from flowers or other sweet food, such as over-ripe fruit, which it sucks up through the proboscis. This food provides energy to fly and reproduce, but most butterflies do not need any body-building foods to see them through their short lives. In fact, a few species have mouthparts that do not open so they cannot feed.

**Purpose**

A general piece of writing describing the main characteristics of all butterflies.

**Audience**

Unknown audience – people who for some reason want to find out about butterflies. Extent of readers' prior knowledge is unknown.

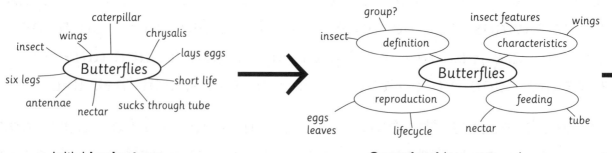

Initial **brainstorm**                    **Organised** into categories

## Organisation and content

*Title:* Straightforward title describing the content.

### Introduction

**Paragraph 1:** definition
    *What are they?* (insects: subset – Lepidoptera)
    *How is this group defined?* (scales; coiled proboscis)
    *How wide is the group?* (worldwide, adapted as necessary)

### Description organised by categories

**Paragraph 2:** characteristics
1  General characteristics shared with all insects;
2  Focus on wings – main characteristic associated with butterflies.

**Paragraph 3:** reproduction
1  Male/female differences;
2  Reproduction and life cycle.

**Paragraph 4:** feeding
1  What/how do they eat?
2  Short life span – little food.

### Conclusion

Paragraph 3 has dealt with life cycle, and paragraph 4
with the imago's short life span – this seems an appropriate place to end.

> # Butterflies
>
> Butterflies belong to the order of insects known as Lepidoptera. This means they have scaly bodies and wings, and a feeding tube on the front of the head, called a proboscis, coiled up when not in use. Their wings may be large, brightly coloured and patterned. Butterflies are found in most parts of the world, and different species are adapted to the environments in which they live.
>
> Like all insects, the butterfly's body is divided into three parts: head, thorax and abdomen. On the head are a pair of antennae, used for smelling, and two large compound eyes. Three pairs of legs and two pairs of wings – fore and hind – grow from the thorax. The wings are made of a very thin membrane, stretched over a framework of 'veins', in the same way as the skin of an umbrella is stretched over the frame. Tiny overlapping scales on the membrane give the wings their pattern and colour.
>
> Male butterflies tend to be more brightly coloured than the females, but the females are larger. They also have bigger wings, enabling them to fly even when they are carrying a heavy burden of eggs. A female butterfly may lay up to 3,000 eggs, always choosing the appropriate plant for the caterpillars to feed on. However, usually only one or two eggs out of a hundred hatch out and many others die as they grow through the stages of larva (caterpillar) and chrysalis (pupa) to become an imago (adult butterfly).
>
> The imago usually has a life span of only a few weeks. It feeds on nectar from flowers or other sweet food, such as over-ripe fruit, which it sucks up through the proboscis. This food provides energy to fly and reproduce, but most butterflies do not need any body-building foods to see them through their short lives. In fact, a few species have mouthparts that do not open so they cannot feed.

---

### Form and style

- Third person report text – a text book extract.
- Non-chronological text, organised according to categories of information.

- Factual writing, covering all important information and a few points of interest.
- General writing about all butterflies, rather than specific facts about a particular species.

---

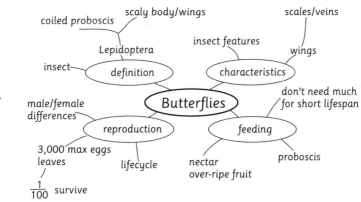

Finished **spidergram** (after research)

---

## Language features

### Generalised language

- Written in the **present tense** – the information is general and ongoing.
- **Generalised participants**, sometimes referred to in the plural (*insects/butterflies*) and sometimes in the 'generalised singular' (*the butterfly's body, a female butterfly, the imago*) where one butterfly is described as if it were a specimen representing the whole group.
- Use of '**weasel words' and phrases** like *tend to be, may be, usually, most.* Terms like this provide a useful 'get-out clause' for the writer when describing a wide ranging group (it's general information with exceptions).
- Use of phrases which indicate how general/specific a particular piece of information is (*Like all insects ..., a few species ...*)

### Formal impersonal language

Text books and encyclopaedias should sound clear and authoritative.

- Written in the **third person**, so we have no idea who the author is.
- Occasional use of the **passive voice** (*insects known as ... Butterflies are found ... the body is divided into three parts*) which is formal and impersonal. However, the use of the passive is limited because the author is also trying to be clear and simple.

- Use of **technical terminology** (*Lepidoptera, proboscis,* etc.) As there is no glossary, the author sometimes tries to clarify the meanings of words which may be unfamiliar, sometimes gambles on the reader knowing the term (*thorax, abdomen, antennae*).

### Descriptive language

Descriptive language in report text differs from the description in stories, poems or even lively recount writing, in that is it concerned only with clarity, not vividness or achieving an emotional response from the reader.

- Many factual **adjectives** (e.g. *scaly bodies ... wings may be large, brightly-coloured and patterned ... tiny, overlapping scales*), concerned with significant detail – often colour, position or size.
- Similarly, extra phrases and clauses often clarify physical features (e.g. *a feeding tube **on the front of the head**, called a proboscis, **coiled up when not in use***).
- Use of **comparison** (*in the same way as the skin of an umbrella ...*), not for effect like a literary simile, but to clarify and aid understanding.
- Where possible, **quantities** and/or **dimensions** are stated (e.g. *up to 3,000 eggs*), but in highly generalised report text, this is often not possible, since individual specimens vary so much.

## Formatted and comparative reports

**Purpose**: to describe what something is like, in a way that draws comparisons or helps the reader see what things have in common.
**Example**: a page from a formatted 'Encyclopaedia of Minibeasts'.

### Text structure

- classification of the particular item;
- information organised to a non-chronological format, allowing comparison between different items;
- description organised according to categories of information;
- basic skeleton framework – a **grid**.

### Language features

- present tense, impersonal writing;
- general nouns/pronouns (not specific people/ things);
- factual writing, often involving technical words and phrases;
- reduced space may mean writing in note form (key words only).

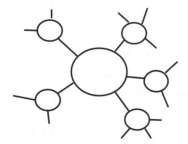

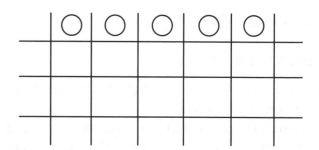

## Key teaching points

- Formatted report text deals with subject matter that can be compared and contrasted, e.g. *British Birds.* The 'spiderleg' categories of a non-comparative report become the headings along one axis of the grid, e.g. *appearance, habitat, feeding habits.* The headings on the other axis are the items to be compared, e.g. *sparrow, chaffinch, swallow.*
- While it seems more complex than non-comparative report, formatted report text is actually easier to teach, as in demonstrating how to write up one of the items you create a template for pupils to write about others.
- Another type of report text which is best planned on a grid is comparative writing (e.g. *Frogs and Toads, Christmas Now and In Victorian Times*), where descriptions of two items are interwoven, with attention to similarities and differences. The

organisation of these texts has much in common with discussion text (see pages 86–91), and may be challenging for apprentice writers.

---

Common forms of **formatted** or **comparative** **report text**:

- information leaflet;
- school project file;
- tourist guide book;
- catalogue;
- magazine article;
- non-fiction book (e.g. geography);
- encyclopaedia entry.

# BUTTERFLY     Scientific name: Lepidoptera

Butterflies are insects with two pairs of brightly-coloured patterned wings. Their bodies and wings are covered in tiny scales – it is the scales that give the wings their pattern. They feed through a tube on the head called a probsocis, which is coiled when not in use.

By travelling from flower to flower to suck up nectar, butterflies help with pollination. They pick up pollen on their abdomen in one flower and it brushes off on another.

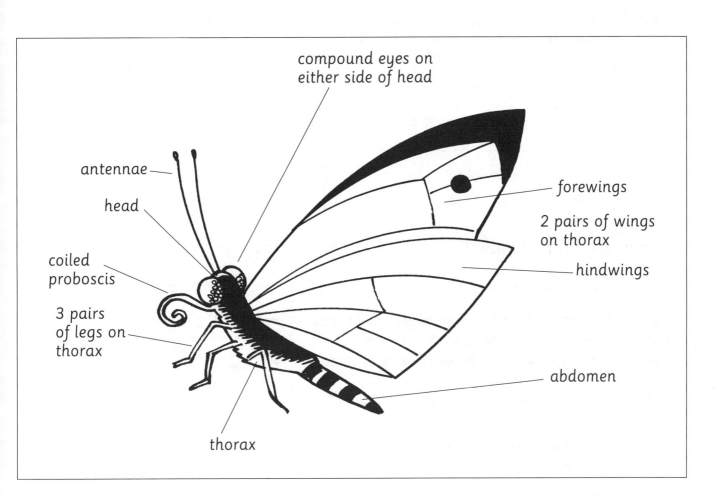

| Habitat | Feeding habits | Life cycle | Predators |
|---|---|---|---|
| Meadows, woodland gardens | Herbivorous: nectar from flowers; ripe fruit | 100s of eggs → caterpillars → pupa → adult (imago) | Birds, bats spiders, lizards, etc. |

<table>
<tr><td>

**Purpose**

1  To create a class encyclopaedia about the minibeasts found around the school.
2  To report information about each creature, based on a research format.

</td><td>

</td><td>

**Audience**

Known audience – members of the same class or school, involved in minibeasts' project.

</td></tr>
</table>

| | Classfication | Key facts | Habitat | Feeding habits | Life cycle | Predators |
|---|---|---|---|---|---|---|
| Butterfly | Insect Lepidoptera | 1. scales and coiled proboscis 2. helps pollination | Meadows woodlands gardens | Herbivorous – nectar ripe fruit | 100s of eggs → caterpillars → pupa → imago | Birds, bats, spiders, frogs, lizards, small mammals |
| Worm | | | | | | |
| Woodlouse | | | | | | |

## Organisation and content

Organisation determined by format.

**Heading:** Name of minibeast, in large capital letters to be seen easily by the reader (this also aids alphabetical organisation of encyclopaedia). Scientific name in italics.

**Main text:** Sentences summing up main facts about butterflies:

1  what distinguishes them from other insects;
2  their importance in plant reproduction.

Written in coherent sentences.

**Picture:** Simplified diagram with labels. Leader lines drawn with ruler (as often as possible leader lines are horizontal). Labels – key words only (print writing style used to differentiate from text)

**Boxed text:** Notes summing up remaining key facts about butterflies: key words only; punctuation, arrows and layout used to clarify meaning.

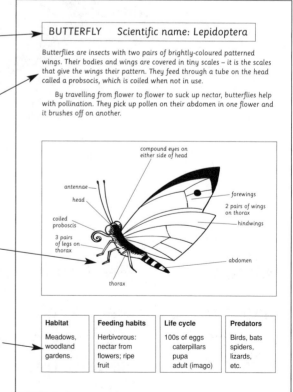

### Form and style

- Report text written to a format.
- Non-chronological text, organised according to agreed categories of information.

- Key facts only, no superfluous detail, but must be clear to readers other than the author – some coherent sentences, some information in note form.

## Language features

### Features of notes

The format is designed to include the maximum information in the minimum space. Labels on the picture and boxed information are therefore in note form. However, these notes must be intelligible to the general reader.

- **Key words,** notably **nouns** and **verbs** (essential adjectives only: *compound eyes, coiled proboscis, ripe fruit*). **Determiners** (including the words *the* and *a*) not used at all.
- Use of **abbreviations** and **symbols** for brevity (*etc.* →). Use of figures rather than words (*3 pairs; 100s of eggs*).
- Use of **punctuation** to clarify meaning in abbreviated text (comma, colon, semicolon).

### Descriptive language

Report text calls for objective, observational description, not vivid, emotional language.

- Factual **adjectives** (e.g. *brightly-coloured patterned wings; tiny scales*), concerned with significant detail – colour, position or size. Description of distinguishing features (... *which is coiled when not in use*).

### Generalised report language

- The information refers to all British butterflies, so the language is highly generalised: **present tense, plural referents** (*butterflies, insects*),
- Language is formal and impersonal: **third person**, so we have no idea who the author is; use of **technical terminology** (*Lepidoptera, proboscis, herbivorous* etc.). In an encyclopaedia of this type, where there is little room for further explanation, one would expect a glossary to clarify unusual technical terms.

## Report writing: stage 1

### Content and organisation

Make a formatted class book based on our *Encyclopaedia of Minibeasts* or another topic of interest (e.g. *Encyclopaedia of British Mammals, Encyclopaedia of Transport*). Create a format for the page, with agreed headings, as in the example on page 55. Demonstrate how to create one page of your book in Shared Writing by:

- using the page format (or a grid, as in our example on page 56) to write rough notes on your chosen topic;
- showing how to draw and label a simplified diagram;
- using the notes to make a neat final page (some sentences, some notes in boxes).

Ask students to use the same page format to research, write notes, draft diagram, then write up their own pages for the book, based on your model.

### Language features

- Writing in sentences – demonstrate how to convert the notes in our exemplar text (page 55) into sentences, e.g. *Butterflies are generally found in meadows, woodlands and gardens.* Discuss the differences between notes and sentences.
- Writing notes, word deletion – demonstrate how to turn our sentences into notes, e.g. *insects – 2 pairs of brightly-coloured wings; tiny scales on body/wings; proboscis (can coil up).*
- Verbs and tense – demonstrate how to use present tense for non-chronological factual writing about general topics, as above. Contrast with recounts (see page 40). Always use present tense on spidergram notes.
- Presentational devices – show how:
  - the uses of headings and subheadings link to the categorisation in a spidergram.
  - writing style can help differentiate parts of the text – capitals for headings, print for labels, joined writing for main text.

### Using spidergrams for non-chronological note-taking

- Ensure students recognise the difference between information that can be organised chronologically and that which can't. In all areas of the curriculum, use spidergrams yourself to illustrate/record the main points of subjects which do not have a chronological basis.
- Encourage students to use this technique to organise their thoughts when planning (e.g. when developing a character or setting for story-writing).
- Use when teaching about key words for note-taking – on a spidergram there isn't room for irrelevance – just enough words to act as an aide memoire.

## Report writing: stage 2

### *Content and organisation*

Demonstrate the links between spidergram notes and organisational devices:

- In reading, investigate how report text is split up into sections (with headings) and sub-sections (with sub-headings). Convert the content into spidergram notes: overall title in the centre; headings on the spider-legs; subheadings radiating from there. Perhaps add key words. Ask children to do the same with other report text material.

- For writing, choose suitable familiar content from any curriculum area to arrange on a spidergram and use as skeleton notes. Discuss organisation, using the spidergram to dictate sections (with headings) and sub-sections (with sub-headings).

### *Language features*

- Verbs and tense – continue to emphasise the use of the present tense, except in historical reports (e.g. 'the Greeks'; 'Victorian clothes') which describe conditions no longer extant.

- Adjectives and adjectival phrases; adverbs of manner – in reading, investigate how adjectives, adjectival phrases and adverbs of manner are used in (a) fiction and poetry (and sometimes recount text): for vividness and effect, to engage and excite the reader (b) non-chronological reports (and most other non-fiction text): to give necessary, factual detail (see notes on pages 53 and 54). In writing non-chronological reports, encourage the use of descriptive words and phrases to give necessary factual detail; demonstrate how to avoid flowery or value-laden description.

## How to BOS

The stages in making a spidergram can be summarised by the acronym BOS:

- **B**rainstorm what you know about the subject. Depending on how familiar you are with the topic, you can do this orally/mentally or jot words and phrases down on paper, in any order. If it's a subject you know nothing at all about, you might start with some research, seeking out key words.
- **O**rganise the material into categories. Think how your facts could be clustered together under headings. Come up with 4–6 main categories, which could then, if necessary, break down into sub-categories. More research may help you choose categories.
- **S**pidergram it. Write the topic title in the middle and the names of the categories at the end of the spider-legs. Then sub-categorise if necessary, or just write relevant key words. Further research will yield more information to note in relevant places.

## Report writing: stage 3

### *Content and organisation*

Notes for a talk: ask students to create their own spidergram notes to use (a) as the basis of writing (b) as a prompt for a prepared talk.

### Paragraphing in reports

- In reading reports, note how the author has decided on paragraph breaks, e.g. in our examples on page 51, ask students to summarise the content of each paragraph.
- Relate to the organisation of notes on a spidergram. Paragraphs are the final stage in the hierarchy: title; sections; sub-sections; paragraphs.
- In a short report text, as page 51, there is no room for headings and subheadings.
- Give students opportunities to research and create spidergram notes for a similar short piece. Discuss how the spidergram will determine paragraphs.

### *Language features*

- Audience and purpose: investigate features of formal impersonal style and the use of 'weasel words' for generalised accounts (see notes on page 53).
- Audience and purpose: contrast the two exemplar texts, discussing how audience and purpose affect layout, writing style, vocabulary.

### Comparative report writing

Another common type of text is the comparative report — text which compares and contrasts two or more items. Like formatted text, this is based on a grid skeleton, but it is then written as coherent text, interweaving the items in the same way as discussion text interweaves points. Enlarge the text below and use to investigate language features of comparative text.

### BUTTERFLY OR MOTH?

Butterflies and moths are two families of creature within the order of insects known as *Lepidoptera* (from the Greek words for 'scaly wings'). This means they have **a great deal in common**: they **both** have scales all over their bodies and wings, giving the wings their characteristic colours and patterns; they **both also** have a proboscis – the feeding tube on the front of their head – which can be coiled up when not in use.

There are **a number of observable differences** between butterflies and moths. **For instance**, **most butterflies** fly by day, **while most moths** fly by night. **Butterflies are, on the whole,** more brightly coloured **whereas moths are more likely** to be shades of brown and grey. **Most butterflies** hold their wings upright over their backs, **while moths tend** to rest with their wings folded flat. **Finally**, butterflies have antennae which are knobbed at the tip; moths' antennae are either feathered or plain.

**There are, however,** about ten thousand species of butterfly in the world, and even more species of moths. Each species is adapted to its habitat, so the variety within both families is enormous. The distinction between the two is an artificial one, decided upon by scientists, and there is no one single feature that separates all butterflies from all moths. **On the whole, the similarities between the two families far outweigh the differences**.

## Report writing: stage 4

### Content and organisation

Ask students to research and plan a non-fiction leaflet on topic of interest:

- use BOSing and research skills to create notes on a spidergram;
- design layout, including headings/subheadings, illustrations, etc.;
- draft each section leaflet, using appropriate style;
- 'publish' leaflet, either in neat handwriting or on computer.

### Language features

- Features of report text: use Reports 1 and 2 and notes on pages 58 and 59 to revise the main language features, including generalised language; factual description; impersonal language; present tense.
- Active and passive: find examples of the passive voice in Report 1. Establish that it is used to maintain an impersonal voice (try transforming into the active, e.g. *We call this order Lepidoptera...You can find butterflies in most parts of the world*). Discuss why an impersonal voice is appropriate in this context.

## Report checklist

### Organisation

- Does the introductory paragraph orientate the reader, so that s/he has a rough idea of what the piece will be about? ☐
- Is the text organised into sections or paragraphs, so that the underlying structure (the way information has been categorised) is clear? ☐
- Is this supported by the layout – headings, subheadings, paragraph breaks? ☐
- Do the closing statements bring the text to a satisfactory conclusion? ☐

### Language features

- Is the text consistently in the present tense (except for historical reports)? ☐
- Is the text written in an appropriately formal, impersonal style (for instance, with occasional use of the passive)? ☐
- Is the style appropriately general? ☐
- If technical vocabulary is used, is its meaning always made clear (as appropriate to the text's audience)? ☐
- Is descriptive language used factually, to describe and clarify, rather than for vividness and effect? ☐
- Are all statements based on fact, rather than value-judgement? ☐

# 3.3 Instruction text

**Purpose**: to tell someone how to do or make something.
**Audience**: general reader who wishes to achieve this purpose (you may have further details about age, interests, etc of audience).

## Text structure

- title or opening sets out **what's to be achieved**;
- starts with **list** of items required;
- often accompanied by **diagram**(s);
- sequenced steps to achieve the goal – what to do, **in time order**;
- skeleton framework – a **flow chart** ('you do this then you do this, etc.').

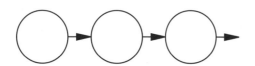

## Language features

- usually written in the **imperative, present** tense;
- in time order (often **numbered** steps and/or **time connectives**);
- all necessary **detail** included (e.g. quantities, spatial directions);
- **clear concise** language, e.g. adjectives and adverbs chosen for clarity rather than vividness and effect;
- the author addresses an anonymous reader, not a named individual.

## Key teaching points

- Simple instruction text is very direct and usually in time sequence. It is thus fairly easy for primary-age children to write. It's a useful vehicle for illustrating the differences between the use of language in fiction and factual writing (e.g. descriptive language chosen for clarity, not vividness) as in report text.
- Sometimes, however, instructions have no particular sequence (as in a list of 'school rules'), so may instead be linked by category.
- Simple instruction text speaks directly to the reader, using imperative verbs (e.g. *Do this, do that*), but more complex instructions are often written in the third person. When more than one person is involved (e.g. in a game), clarity requires that they be named (e.g. *Player A, the batting team*) and their actions described impersonally. This links instruction writing to the type of impersonal language used in explanations and discussions.
- In the early stages of learning to write instructions, it's essential that students have actually carried out the process concerned before they write. For this reason, cross-curricular links to art, design, information technology and PE are invaluable.
- Diagrams are often necessary to make instructions clear. Instruction writing is an opportunity to introduce the skills of drawing and labelling diagrams.

---

Common forms of **instruction text**:

- recipe;
- technical manual (e.g. for car, computer);
- non-fiction book (e.g. sports skills, art);
- timetable, route-finder;
- list of rules;
- posters, notices, signs;
- sewing or knitting pattern;
- instructions on packaging (e.g. cooking or washing instructions).

# How to make a papier mâché bowl

You need:   half a cup of flour
half a cup of water
a tablespoon of salt
a container for mixing paste
a balloon, blown-up and knotted
a strip of card (about 30 cm by 4 cm)
sticky tape and scissors
paint and brushes
varnish and brush

*Papier mâché* is the French for 'chewed paper'! It is a mixture of paper and paste that hardens when dry.

1   First make the paste. Put the flour and salt into the container and gradually mix in the water until it is thick and creamy.

2   Dip the strips of newspaper into the paste and smooth them down on to the unknotted end of the balloon. Cover enough of the balloon to make a bowl shape. Use three or four layers of paper strips. Leave to dry.

3   Make a base for the bowl by taping the card into a circle shape, and taping it on to the balloon. Cover with a few more pasted strips to hold it in place.

4   Pop the balloon and remove its plastic skin. Ask a grown-up to help you trim the top of the bowl, and smooth more pasted strips over the edges to finish it off. Leave to dry.

5   Paint the bowl in bright colours. When it is dry brush on a final coat of varnish.

**Purpose**
To help the reader achieve this aim easily and safely.

**Audience**
Readers (probably children) who want to know how to make a papier mâché bowl.

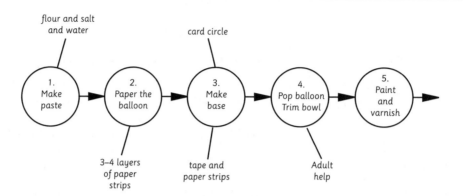

flour and salt and water

card circle

| 1. Make paste | 2. Paper the balloon | 3. Make base | 4. Pop balloon Trim bowl | 5. Paint and varnish |

3–4 layers of paper strips

tape and paper strips

Adult help

## Organisation and content

*Title:* a statement of what is to be achieved. This is reinforced and clarified by the illustration at the foot of the page.

### List of equipment

- provided first, so that the reader can ensure that everything is available before starting the process;
- items listed vertically (and in order of use) for easy reading and checking.

### Boxed information

Extra information (explaining a term likely to be unfamiliar to readers) is held separate from the rest of the text, so that it does not interfere with the clarity of the instructions.

### Sequenced instructions

**Numbered steps aid clarity.** These act like paragraphs in other texts: their spatial arrangement helps the reader break up the information into manageable chunks.

Each numbered step sums up an important stage in the process:

1  Making the paste.
2  Papering the balloon.
3  Making a base.
4  Finishing the bowl.
5  Painting and varnishing.

### Illustration

Illustration of final product helps the reader understand exactly what is to be achieved. Further diagrams throughout the text would also aid comprehension, but were omitted for teaching purposes.

---

### How to make a papier mâché bowl

You need:   half a cup of flour
            half a cup of water
            a tablespoon of salt
            a container for mixing paste
            a balloon, blown-up and knotted
            a strip of card (about 30 cm by 4 cm)
            sticky tape and scissors
            paint and brushes
            varnish and brush

*Papier mâché* is the French for chewed paper ! It is a mixture of paper and paste that hardens when dry.

1  First make the paste. Put the flour and salt into the container and gradually mix in the water until it is thick and creamy.

2  Dip the strips of newspaper into the paste and smooth them down on to the unknotted end of the balloon. Cover enough of the balloon to make a bowl shape. Use three or four layers of paper strips. Leave to dry.

3  Make a base for the bowl by taping the card into a circle shape, and taping it on to the balloon. Cover with a few more pasted strips to hold it in place.

4  Pop the balloon and remove its plastic skin. Ask a grown-up to help you trim the top of the bowl, and smooth more pasted strips over the edges to finish it off. Leave to dry.

5  Paint the bowl in bright colours. When it is dry brush on a final coat of varnish.

**Form and style**

- Instruction text – clear, simple, speaking directly to the reader; no unnecessary detail.
- Successful outcome, equipment required, and all steps in the process must be included.
- Layout must illustrate sequence – would diagrams help?

---

## Language features

### Addressing the reader

- Written in the **imperative present tense**, to speak directly to the reader as s/he carries out the instructions.
- The imperative is always in the **second person** (e.g. *you* in step 4), which applies generally to all readers. All references to people are generalised rather than specific (e.g. *a grown-up* in step 4). When instructions are given in the **third person** (see Key teaching point 2 on page 62), these are generalised human agents – e.g. *Player A, the batting team* – rather than specific participants.
- There are many short simple sentences (*First make the paste.*) and compound sentences where two ideas are simply linked by *and*. This mirrors the simple language patterns of speech, as though the writer were talking directly to the reader.

### Clarity and relevance

Instructions must be totally clear.

- In the list of equipment, **quantities** and/or **dimensions** are stated explicitly where necessary.
- **Necessary detail** is provided but no superfluous detail (e.g. the list specifies that the balloon is *blown up and knotted* but doesn't mention, for instance, the colour of the balloon, which is irrelevant).

- Use of the **imperative** means that the verb is usually at the beginning of the sentence, which gives it prominence. The verbs are chosen for maximum clarity, not for descriptive effect (e.g. *make, mix, dip*).
- **Adverbs** and **adjectives** are included for clarification, not for effect (e.g. **gradually** *mix in the water until it is* **thick** *and* **creamy**). All these descriptive words are necessary to the reader's understanding of the instructions. There is no value-laden description (e.g. *lovely and thick*) or vivid, descriptive language (e.g. *languorously, disgusting*).
- **Simple language patterns** (mainly simple and compound sentences, see above).

### Sequence

- **Numbers** clearly indicate the sequence of the steps (see *Sequenced instructions,* opposite).
- These are backed up occasionally by **sequential connectives** (*First, when*).

### Awareness of audience

The readers of these instructions are likely to be children. Simplicity and clarity (see above) are therefore doubly important.

- There is also an assumption that the reader will need help with areas which could be a safety issue (*Ask a grown-up to help you trim...*).

## Instruction writing: stage 1

### Content and organisation

Focus on presentational devices:

- See *'Numbers, lists, pictures, boxes'*, below.
- Investigate pictures and diagrams in instruction text, and help students recognise the need for simplicity and clear labelling. Give opportunities for drawing and evaluating diagrams.

### Language features

- Use of adjectives: compare the adjectives used in instructions (e.g. our example) to those in fiction and poetry; help students recognise the different way language is used depending on purpose and audience.
- Second person verbs: provide a list of verbs (e.g. *to eat, to sing, to smile, to throw)* and ask pupils to use them in an instruction (e.g. *Eat your dinner.*) Discuss who is being addressed on each occasion (i.e. *you*... the second person). Talk about 1st/2nd/3rd person and make a list of sentences for each verb, e.g. *I eat my dinner; you eat your dinner; he eats his dinner.*

## Numbers, lists, pictures, boxes

- Provide students with a range of instruction texts, preferably genuine published material:
  - books of recipes, craft ideas, science activities
  - magazine cuttings: DIY ideas, recipes
  - rules: school rules, rules for games, membership of clubs
  - instructions for using household equipment: packaging, labels, manuals
  - signs and notices, e.g. *Keep off the grass, Keep out, Take your litter home with you*
  - travel instructions, e.g. timetables, route-finders, map books.
- Discuss the range of organisational and presentational devices (e.g. *Why do you think they've put this bit in a box? What's the point of using capitals here? Why is there such a lot of space around this bit?*). Help students see that clarity and simplicity are crucial to instructions.
- Ask students in pairs to copy, photocopy or (if it's expendable material) cut out at least one good example of a presentational device, and make it into a mini-poster, with a caption explaining (a) what it is, including the correct terminology (b) why it is helpful in instruction text.
- Each pair can then explain their findings to the rest of the class, and their mini-posters can be compiled into a collage.

## Instruction writing: stage 2

### Content and organisation

- Help students recognise that conventional instructions consist of four elements: title, list, diagram(s) and staged steps. In shared reading, help them see how the staged steps can be converted into a simple flow chart containing key words (as in our example, page 64).

- When they are learning a new skill – in art, PE, IT, etc. – encourage students to create a simple flowchart of the stages with memory-joggers for each stage in a 'bubble'. If you keep the bubbles small, it will encourage them to keep key words down to a minimum. The flowchart can act as an aide memoire but also, if necessary, as content for instruction writing.

- 'Tell the Alien'. Ask students to imagine they are aliens visiting earth and reporting back on how other aliens can blend in seamlessly with earthlings. They should create skeleton instructions for an everyday activity (e.g. taking a shower, eating spaghetti) and use them to create 'audio-instructions' to deliver to the class.

### Language features

- Adverbs: as with adjectives (see Stage 1) note the different ways adverbs are used in instructions and fiction/poetry.

- Verbs: person, imperative mood. With pupils create a selection of second person statements (e.g. *You can sing*.), questions (*Can you sing?*) and commands (*Sing!*). Display them on labelled posters, and add the word *imperative* to the third: *Commands (imperative)*. Explain the connection between this word and *emperor, imperial, imperious*. Notice the differences between the three types of sentence in terms of their meaning and their grammar: word order and punctuation. Note that not all statements/questions can be converted into the imperative. Find examples of each kind of sentence in shared texts – note the preponderance of imperatives in instruction writing.

### First, next, then, finally

Video part of a TV cookery programme and count the number of times the presenter says 'and then'…or just 'then' while demonstrating a recipe. Establish that the presenter uses this simple connective to show s/he is moving from one step in the process to another. Connectives are like signposts to the audience: 'I've finished that bit…now we're on to something else.'

'And then' is a common connective in speech, when we are in the same place as our audience and they can actually see what we are doing. In written language, the repeated use of 'and then' is boring to read, and actually makes the text less, rather than more, clear. Collect alternative ways of signalling the move between steps from recipe and craft books, including: numbering, bullet points, sequential connectives, paragraphing and layout.

Ask pupils to return to some instruction text they made earlier, and improve the coherence by better use of these connective devices.

## Instruction writing: stage 3

### *Content and organisation*

#### Plan it, make it, write it, test it

- In Design and Technology, ask students to design and make an artefact of some kind from scratch. They should think through the design stages carefully in advance, and create a simple flowchart of the steps they intend to follow (see 'Stage 2' notes). They could also create a diagram of the finished artefact, as they intend it to look.
- As they carry out the activity, the flow-chart/diagram may be changed and annotated, as plans and outcomes change. This provides a working record of the activity, which can be kept as evidence in their DT folder.
- The flowchart can also be used as skeleton notes for writing instructions. Students' experience of making the artefact means they have expert knowledge of the content of the instructions. In shared reading, concentrate on organisational and linguistic features of instruction text.
- Bearing this in mind, students should write up instructions for making their artefacts, proof-reading and editing them for clarity. The instructions can be placed in a hat, and during the next DT lesson, each student should draw out a set of instructions to read and follow. Readers can then feed back to writers.

### *Language features*

- Verbs – tense, imperative, persons transformations:
  - Make an enlarged copy of the text in the box (our example text converted into a recount). Read with the children and ask which would be easier to follow if you wanted to make a bowl: recount or instructions? Discuss (a) why (b) the differences in tense and person between the two texts.
  - Establish that one of the main effects of the imperative is to emphasise the verbs (which are critical in instructions) by bringing them upfront.
  - Ask pupils to convert sections of instruction text to recount and vice versa.

#### Our papier mâché bowl

First we made the paste. We put the flour and salt into the container and gradually mixed in the water until it was thick and creamy. Then we dipped the strips of newspaper into the paste and smoothed them down on to the unknotted end of the balloon. We covered enough of the balloon to make a bowl shape, using three or four layers of paper strips. Then we left it to dry.

We made a base for the bowl by taping the card into a circle shape and taping it on to the balloon. We covered it with a few more pasted strips to hold it in place. Next we popped the balloon and removed its plastic skin. Mrs Bruce helped us trim the top of the bowl, and we smoothed more pasted strips over the edges to finish it off, then left it to dry.

Finally, we painted the bowl in bright colours. When it was dry, we brushed on a final coat of varnish.

## Instruction writing: stage 4

### Content and organisation

- Revise the four-part nature of instruction text: informative title, list of what's required, staged instructions (which can be represented as a simple flow chart), diagram(s). Revisit the organisational and presentational devices that can be used, including numbering, layout, headings and bullets.
- Introduce more complex instructions, involving the actions of more than one person (e.g. players, teams). Ask students to choose a game or sport they know well and create skeleton instructions for how to play it. This can be an extremely challenging task, with skeleton notes as complex as those for our explanation example.

### Language features

- **Impersonal writing**: When instructions are too complex for simple imperative, they must be written in the third person. The writer has to devise names for participants (e.g. *Player A, Player B; the striker, the keeper*). This means ensuring the reader has any necessary information about each (often given in a box, so as not to interfere with the clarity of the instructions).
- **Sequence and clarity**: The writing of complex instructions involves clear sequencing (sometimes including terms such as *meanwhile*). It also requires clarity in terms of technical vocabulary, which may need definition.
- Use checklist below to revise major language features.

---

### Instruction checklist

#### Organisation

- Does the title (or opening) set out what's to be achieved? ☐
- If equipment or ingredients are required, are these given in a clear list? ☐
- Is there a series of sequenced steps to achieve the goal/process? ☐
- Does the layout and presentation make the sequence clear and easy to follow? ☐
- If appropriate, is there a clearly labelled diagram (or diagrams)? ☐
- Are other organisational devices used for clarity, e.g. boxes for extra information or tips, bullet points, numbers? ☐

#### Language features

- Is the text consistently in the imperative present tense (except when there is more than one person/team involved)? ☐
- If more than one person/team is involved, are they named or labelled in some way so they are clearly distinguishable? ☐
- Is the language and vocabulary clear and concise? ☐
- Are quantities and measurements clearly stated wherever necessary? ☐
- Is descriptive language used for clarity rather than vividness or effect? ☐
- Are time connectives or other devices used to ensure that the sequence of the stages is clear? ☐

# 3.4 Explanation text

**Purpose:** to explain how or why something happens.
**Example:** an extract from a science textbook.

## Text structure

- title often asks a question or defines the process to be explained;
- text usually opens with general statement(s) to introduce the topic;
- a series of logical steps explaining the process, usually in time order;
- often accompanied by **diagram**(s);
- basic skeleton framework – a **flow chart** ('this happens, leading to this, which leads to this', etc.).

## Language features

- **present tense** (the process is general);
- **time connectives** and other devices to aid chronological structure;
- **causal connectives** and other devices demonstrating **cause and effect**.

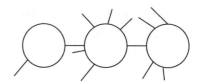

## Key teaching points

- Explanations are difficult to write. Before putting pen to paper, students must thoroughly understand the process they are about to explain. Making a skeleton framework first – especially a flowchart and/or labelled diagram – develops understanding.

- However, even making the flowchart can be tricky! There are many possible variations, depending upon the process in question, e.g.

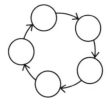

a **cycle**

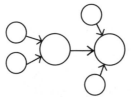

**multiple causes** and/or effects

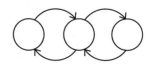

**reversible** effects

- Students need to see plenty of models created by the teacher. They also need time to experiment with different ways of representing a process (collaborative work is particularly useful). However, the process of developing a suitable skeleton framework can in itself aid understanding.

- When students come to write, encourage them to include flowchart(s) or diagram(s) alongside their text. Most explanation is enhanced by visual representation (e.g. the exemplar text opposite would be easier to understand if the flowchart on page 64 were provided alongside, but this was omitted for teaching purposes.)

---

Forms of text which may be **explanations**:

- textbook;
- encyclopaedia entry;
- non-fiction book (e.g. geography, biology);
- technical manual (e.g. for car, dishwasher);
- 'question and answer' articles and leaflets;
- write-up of science experiment.

# Why do people die if they stop breathing?

In order to stay alive, human beings need a constant supply of **oxygen** (a gas found in the air) to all parts of the body. They also need to rid their bodies of a waste gas called **carbon dioxide**, which would otherwise poison them.

These two gases are carried round the body in the blood. **Veins** carry blood to the heart and **arteries** carry blood away from the heart. Both divide into millions of tiny **capillary blood vessels**. Gases can move between the blood in the capillaries and the tiny **cells** which make up the human body.

When a human being breathes in, the air goes down into the **lungs**, which are like two spongy bags filled with millions of air sacs. Oxygen from the air passes through the sacs into the capillary blood vessels. The blood then carries the oxygen through a vein to the **heart**.

The heart pumps this oxygen-carrying blood around the whole body through arteries, and these divide into capillaries to reach the body cells. Oxygen passes from the blood to the cells, and carbon dioxide (the waste gas) passes from the cells into the blood. Veins take this waste-carrying blood back to the heart, which pumps it back to the lungs. There the carbon dioxide passes into the air sacs.

When the human being breathes out, the carbon dioxide is pushed back out into the air. Breathing in and out is therefore essential because it ensures that life-giving oxygen is constantly replaced and poisonous carbon dioxide expelled.

**Purpose**

1 To provide the answer as simply and clearly as possible.

2 To explain the roles of the lungs, heart, and circulation of the blood in maintaining life.

**Audience**

Readers who want to know the answer to the question in the title, but who know little about the subject.

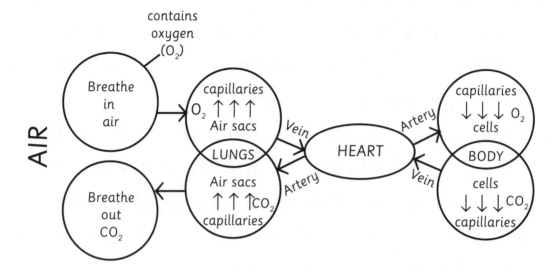

## Organisation and content

*Title:* a question requiring an explanation of a process.

### Introduction

**Paragraph 1:** general statement of why we breathe

1 one sentence about oxygen
2 one sentence about carbon dioxide.

**Paragraph 2:** defines some key terms (veins, arteries, capillary blood vessels) to be used in the explanation. Giving these definitions in advance means the explanation can proceed more smoothly.

### Explanation

**Paragraph 3:** the first three stages in the process, taking oxygen from the air, through the blood to the heart (as shown in the flowchart above).

**Paragraph 4:** the next three stages in the process, returning the blood to the lungs (as shown in the flow-chart above).

### Conclusion

**Final paragraph:** concluding statement of why we breathe

1 first sentence: conclusion of the process
2 second sentence: summary of the answer to the question.

### Why do people die if they stop breathing?

In order to stay alive, human beings need a constant supply of **oxygen** (a gas found in the air) to all parts of the body. They also need to rid their bodies of a waste gas called **carbon dioxide**, which would otherwise poison them.

These two gases are carried round the body in the blood. **Veins** carry blood to the heart and **arteries** carry blood away from the heart. Both divide into millions of tiny **capillary blood vessels**. Gases can move between the blood in the capillaries and the tiny **cells** which make up the human body.

When a human being breathes in, the air goes down into the **lungs**, which are like two spongy bags filled with millions of air sacs. Oxygen from the air passes through the sacs into the capillary blood vessels. The blood then carries the oxygen through a vein to the **heart**.

The heart pumps this oxygen-carrying blood around the whole body through arteries, and these divide into capillaries to reach the body cells. Oxygen passes from the blood to the cells, and carbon dioxide (the waste gas) passes from the cells into the blood. Veins take this waste-carrying blood back to the heart, which pumps it back to the lungs. There the carbon dioxide passes into the air sacs.

When the human being breathes out, the carbon dioxide is pushed back out into the air. Breathing in and out is therefore essential because it ensures that life-giving oxygen is constantly replaced and poisonous carbon dioxide expelled.

---

**Form and style**

- Explanation text – general, impersonal, formal, but also clear and simple.
- Technical terminology must be explained.

- Layout must illustrate sequence – paragraphs; would diagrams or pictures help?

---

## Language features

### General language

- Written in the **present tense** because this is a general process, happening time and time again.
- It refers to *human beings* (a general term), not just specific named people.

### Formal, impersonal language

Explanations should sound clear and authoritative, not personal and chatty. They should:

- be written in the **third person** (*human beings/they* – not we);
- occasionally use the passive voice (e.g. *gases are carried, oxygen is constantly replaced*) which is formal and impersonal. However, the use of the passive is limited because it can be difficult to understand (the author has tried to balance formality and clarity);
- frequently use formal, **technical terminology** (see below) rather than simplified language;
- use **complex sentences** (see 'Cause and effect' below) which are a feature of formal written language.

### Technical terminology

Technical terms are necessary for accuracy but must be defined for the non-technical reader. In the absence of a glossary, the author uses a number of techniques to provide information:

- brackets: *oxygen* (*a gas found in the air*);
- explanation given before the noun: *a waste gas called carbon dioxide*;
- explanatory subordinate clause: *which would otherwise poison them*;
- an entire paragraph (paragraph 2) providing definitions of words to be used later.

### Sequence

Processes usually involve a sequence of events:

- **sequential connectives** (*When..., then*) help to indicate the stages in the sequence;
- **paragraph breaks** indicate significant stages, but cohesion between paragraphs must be maintained (e.g. *The blood then carries the oxygen.../The heart pumps this oxygen-carrying blood...*).

### Cause and effect

- **Causal connectives** (*In order to..., When..., therefore..., because...*).
- **Complex sentences** show the interrelationships between the ideas expressed in each clause.
- Clear links between the **title**, the **opening statement** and the final sentence, which is a **summary** of the explanation, providing the answer to the question.

## Explanation writing: stage 1

### *Content and organisation*

Focus on how to make flowcharts.

- Investigate flowcharts and diagrams in published texts (see list on page 70), noting how few words authors need to use when they combine them with graphic organisers and illustrations.
- Make flowcharts to help explain processes in other curricular areas (see below).

### *Language features*

#### Words and pictures

- Provide a flowchart or diagram for a familiar process without any accompanying labels or explanatory text. Discuss with pupils and ask them to help you provide labels/minimum text to make it clear to a reader.
- Discuss the sort of words you have used. (Generally, labels consist mainly of nouns and verbs.) Discuss any other symbols you have used, e.g. arrows, and what they mean.
- Now ask them to explain the process in words for someone who is unable to see your diagram/flowchart. Discuss how language changes when the visual display is absent and the burden of explanation falls completely on the words.

#### Making flowcharts

- Whenever possible, and throughout your teaching, demonstrate how to construct flowcharts and diagrams to help you explain (and students understand) processes in all curriculum areas. Don't be afraid to change/improve on flowcharts as you go on. It's difficult to get them right first time, and students should know this.
- Use a variety of forms of flowcharts (e.g. cycles, reversible flowcharts – see examples on page 72) so students see that this type of skeleton is very flexible, and depends on the process concerned.
- Display flowcharts and diagrams in the classroom as part of cross-curricular work.
- Give students the chance to try their own. Choose a familiar process from any curricular area. Ask them, in pairs, to design a flow chart and/or diagram to represent it. Encourage students to draft and redraft if necessary, and to create final tidy versions. Discuss the success (or otherwise) of their efforts. On the basis of the most successful, create an effective shared version.

## Explanation writing: stage 2

### *Content and organisation*

- Continue to discuss the audience and purpose of explanation texts in shared reading and how this affects the layout, presentation, structure and organisation of the text.
- In particular, discuss the significance of:
  - accompanying illustrations and diagrams;
  - headed sections, bullet-pointing, numbering of points; why has the author chosen to use particular organisational features in each case?
- Diagrams versus pictures. The skeleton flow-chart on page 72 looks very complicated. Two ways to make it easier to understand would be:
  - to turn it into a more recognisable picture (i.e. a human body);
  - to use colour-coding (red for oxygenated blood; blue for waste-carrying blood); ask students to try converting it into a simplified, colour-coded picture, using the written explanation to help.

### *Language features*

- Key features of explanation text. Draw attention to these in shared reading (see notes on our example on page 71). Focus especially on:
  - present tense (because this is a general and frequently repeated process);
  - sequential connectives and paragraphing, indicating sequence of events;
  - formal tone (third person impersonal writing, technical terminology);
  - causal language and punctuation (see activity below).

## Making causal connections

- From reading collect a range of connectives and language constructions that indicate cause and effect, such as:
  - conjunctions (used to join clauses within a sentence), e.g. **because, so, if** (this happens, something else follows), **when** (this happens, something follows);
  - sentence connectives (used to make links between two sentences), e.g. **therefore, consequently, as a result**;
  - sentence openings: **the reason ... is that ... this results in ... this causes...**.
- Display these words/phrases/clauses and ask pupils to invent silly sentences (or more than one sentence if necessary) using them, e.g. *The reason our cat is fat is that she eats one buffalo a day; When I hear Zac Ephron, my hair turns purple.*
- Use the examples to discuss how the constructions work, appropriate punctuation, and any other issues, e.g. the accepted standard form is '*the reason...*' not '*the reason **why**...*'
- Collect the best silly sentences and ask pupils to illustrate them (before and after pictures) to make into wall posters.
- Display the posters with the causal words and punctuation highlighted. Encourage pupils to use these constructions as models in explanatory writing.

## Explanation writing: stage 3

### *Content and organisation*

- Discuss how purpose and audience affects the layout, presentation, structure and organisation of the explanation text, as covered in 'stage 2'.
- Choose a process familiar to pupils from another curricular area and, with the class compile a flowchart/diagram/simplified picture to illustrate it. Discuss how the organisational features mentioned above might be used in writing up the explanation.

### *Language features*

- Look at examples of explanation text to revise key language features covered in stage 2: generalised language (present tense, third person); sequential links; causal connectives and constructions; technical vocabulary (see below);
- Spoken and written language; impersonal style. Cover the text and ask students to explain particular parts of it in their own words. (If possible record these to hear again.) Contrast spoken and written versions, and discuss why they differ:
  - spoken language takes place in shared context – often interactive – where the speaker can use gesture, intonation and references to pictures etc. to convey meaning;
  - written explanations require conciseness, clarity and organisation (often into complex sentences);
  - spoken language is personal, and therefore informal; written explanations must be more authoritative and therefore impersonal (e.g. passive voice).

## Clear, concise and informative

- Ask students in groups to collect at least six reasonably familiar technical terms from geography, history, science, maths, PE, music.
- Pairs of students should then take a word each and provide (a) a glossary definition (b) a sentence which uses the word in context.
- Try a quiz, group against group, in which students read out (a) their definitions (b) their sentences, but with the word bleeped out, for others to guess.
- While investigating the language of explanation texts (see above), focus on technical terminology and the ways an author explains the meaning of technical words used within the text (see notes on page 73).
- Look for further techniques for ensuring clarity in other examples of explanation text.
- Ask students to return to their own definitions/sentences. Can they integrate their definition into their sentence (shortening and simplifying it if necessary)?

## Explanation writing: stage 4

### Content and organisation

Continue to revise organisational features (see 'stages 2 and 3') in shared reading, and check comprehension by converting texts into flowcharts/diagrams. Use flowcharts/diagrams of processes from other subject areas to provide content for explanatory writing.

### Language features

- Active and passive: demonstrate **orally** how to convert passive sentences (e.g. *These two gases are carried round the body in the blood*) into the active (*The blood carries these two gases round the body*) and vice versa (active: *Veins carry blood to the heart*; passive: *Blood is carried to the heart by veins*). Ask students to try the same activity with silly made-up sentences. Discuss how the passive contributes to explanations:
  - it is more impersonal and thus more authoritative;
  - you can avoid reference to the agent of an action (*The plant was watered regularly*), whereas in the active the agent must be stated (*We watered the plant).*
- Formal language: see 'Report writing: stage 3'.

---

## Explanation checklist

### Organisation

- Is there a clear title which introduces the process to be explained? ☐
- If appropriate, are there clear sections with subheadings? ☐
- Does the text open with a general statement, introducing the topic? ☐
- Is there a series of logical steps, explaining the process? ☐
- If possible, is this in time order? ☐
- Have you used organisational devices such as bullet points where appropriate? ☐
- Are well-labelled diagrams used where appropriate to make the meaning clear? ☐
- Is the explanation supported by the positioning of paragraph breaks? ☐
- Is there a closing statement, bringing the explanation to a satisfactory conclusion? ☐

### Language features

- Is the text consistently in the present tense? ☐
- Is the text impersonal and authoritative – written in the third person, with use of the passive where appropriate? ☐
- Are there time connectives and other devices to show the sequential structure? ☐
- Is technical terminology used clearly and concisely and, where necessary, defined for the audience? ☐
- Are causal connectives and other devices used to show cause and effect? ☐

# 3.5 Persuasion text

**Purpose**: to argue the case for a **point of view**.
**Example**: an editorial from a spoof newspaper.

## Text structure

- opening **statement of the case** to be argued;
- arguments, given in the form of **point + elaboration**;
- elaboration may be **evidence, explanation, examples**;
- conclusion: **reiteration** of the case and **summary of the points**;
- skeleton framework – **pronged bullet points**.

## Language features

- **present** tense, usually **generic** participants;
- **logical** language constructions and connectives;
- **persuasive devices**, often including emotive **and rhetorical** language.

## Key teaching points

- 'Persuasion' covers a wide range of text types, from a simple (and highly visual) advertisement to a carefully argued letter of complaint. All, however, conform to the '**point, elaboration**' format. In the advertisement the point is probably made with a visual image or a slogan, and elaboration consists of design, colour, wordplay, and so on. In the letter of complaint the elaboration may be:
  - **further details** or **explanation**;
  - **evidence** or **argument**;
  - **examples**.
- When reading persuasion text, students should be alerted to the difference between **fact** and **opinion**, and encouraged to question writers' presentation of 'facts' and use of persuasive devices (see page 81). They should also be aware of fact and opinion in composing their own arguments.

- When writing persuasion, students should consider what they want their readers to do as a result of reading the piece. A clear idea of a **projected outcome** clarifies planning.
- Older students benefit from opportunities to research and argue points about which they do not feel strongly, or with which they actually disagree.

Common forms of **persuasion text**:

- advertisement;
- catalogue;
- travel brochure;
- pamphlet from pressure group;
- political manifesto;
- newspaper or magazine article;
- poster or flier;
- book blurb;
- letter to the editor or editorial.

# Time to give Mary the chop

Last week it was proved beyond any shadow of doubt that Mary Stuart, the former Queen of Scots, has been plotting yet again against the life of our dear queen, Elizabeth. It is clearly difficult for our beloved monarch to consent to her own cousin's death, but after nineteen years of threat and betrayal, surely the time has come to sign Mary's death warrant?

The foolish Queen of Scots was long ago rejected by her own countrymen. During her brief but turbulent reign, Scotland suffered religious unrest, lack of leadership and eventually a bloody civil war. As a result, the Scottish people took away her crown and threw her into prison. When she escaped and fled to England, all Scotland sighed with relief to be rid of her!

Since then Mary has lived under Queen Elizabeth's generous protection – and at the expense of English taxpayers – in comfortable English country houses. She has given nothing in return. On the contrary, she has taken every possible opportunity to plot against Elizabeth's life! Surely such betrayal cannot be tolerated any longer?

Moreover, as long as Mary lives, there will be plots. This woman has always claimed to be the rightful Queen of England, and she has always had the support of the King of Spain, who knows he can make her his puppet. Could any true Englishman want to exchange our wise, generous Elizabeth for this vain, selfish woman? Could anyone want our free, prosperous country to fall under the control of the power-crazed King of Spain?

It is hard for Elizabeth to sign the document that sends her own flesh and blood to the block. Yet sign it she must – for herself, for justice, and for the future of England.

from 'The Tudor Times', 1587

### Purpose

To convince readers that Mary Queen of Scots should be executed. This involves:

- gaining their attention;
- gaining their trust;
- convincing them of the importance of the argument and the rightness of the cause.

**+**

### Audience

Newspaper readers (unknown audience). Only the most basic background knowledge can be assumed.

### Projected outcome

*What do I want my audience to do?*
Support this point of view; help convince Queen Elizabeth to sign the death warrant.

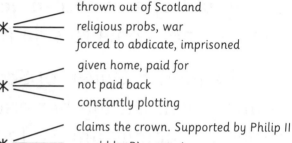

Mary is trouble
* thrown out of Scotland
religious probs, war
forced to abdicate, imprisoned

She has betrayed us
* given home, paid for
not paid back
constantly plotting

If plots succeed Spain takes over
* claims the crown. Supported by Philip II
would be P's puppet.
England falls to Spain

## Organisation and content

*Title:* newspaper headline (short, snappy, eye-catching).

### Introductory paragraph

Setting out (a) the argument: Mary has betrayed Elizabeth again and must die (b) the problem: Elizabeth is reluctant to have her executed.

### Argument

**Paragraph 2: point 1** – Mary has already failed Scotland.
**Elaboration** = evidence: problems during her reign; Scots threw her out.

**Paragraph 3: point 2** – Mary has betrayed Elizabeth (and the English taxpayers)
**Elaboration** = explanation: she's been given a home; in return she has plotted against her benefactors.

**Paragraph 4: point 3** – As long as Mary lives there will be plots, and if she succeeds the outcome will be terrible.
**Elaboration** = contrast between Elizabeth and Mary as queen.

### Conclusion

**Final paragraph:** Reiteration: summary of problem; simplified summary of the arguments.

---

### Time to give Mary the chop

Last week it was proved beyond any shadow of doubt that Mary Stuart, the former Queen of Scots, has been plotting yet again against the life of our dear queen, Elizabeth. It is clearly difficult for our beloved monarch to consent to her own cousin's death, but after nineteen years of threat and betrayal, surely the time has come to sign Mary's death warrant?

The foolish Queen of Scots was long ago rejected by her own countrymen. During her brief but turbulent reign, Scotland suffered religious unrest, lack of leadership and eventually a bloody civil war. As a result, the Scottish people took away her crown and threw her into prison. When she escaped and fled to England, all Scotland sighed with relief to be rid of her!

Since then Mary has lived under Queen Elizabeth's generous protection – and at the expense of English taxpayers – in comfortable English country houses. She has given nothing in return. On the contrary, she has taken every possible opportunity to plot against Elizabeth's life! Surely such betrayal cannot be tolerated any longer?

Moreover, as long as Mary lives, there will be plots. This woman has always claimed to be the rightful Queen of England, and she has always had the support of the King of Spain, who knows he can make her his puppet. Could any true Englishman want to exchange our wise, generous Elizabeth for this vain, selfish woman? Could anyone want our free, prosperous country to fall under the control of the power-crazed King of Spain?

It is hard for Elizabeth to sign the document that sends her own flesh and blood to the block. Yet sign it she must – for herself, for justice, and for the future of England.

*from 'The Tudor Times', 1587*

## Form and style

- persuasion text – a newspaper editorial;
- a reasoned argument containing several points, each backed up by evidence or further argument;
- persuasive language and logic;
- emotive language, to draw the reader along with the cause.

## Language features

### General language

- Apart from historical references, written in the **present tense**, because the issue is a current one for the writer.
- A mixture of named people (*Mary, Elizabeth, Philip of Spain* and the generalised participants who are affected by their actions (*Her own countrymen, the English taxpayers, any true Englishman...*).

### Formal impersonal language

An editorial requires formal language, suggesting that the arguments have been carefully considered. Formality also helps deflect attention from shaky logic or evidence, and can be used to disguise opinion as fact.

- Written in the **third person**, with no indication of who the author is.
- Occasional use of the **passive voice** (e.g. *It was proved, such betrayal cannot be tolerated*) which is formal and impersonal.
- Use of **formal vocabulary** (e.g. *monarch, Moreover*).

### The language of argument

The argument consists of an opening premise, then three supporting points (see 'Arguments', opposite), held together by logical language:

- Complex sentences using **logical connectives** of the *if... then* type (*after nineteen years... it is time...; When she escaped... all Scotland must...*).
- **Connectives** between sentences showing logical relationships:
  - *As a result* indicates cause and effect.
  - *On the contrary... Yet...* showing this

sentence will state something in opposition to the proceeding one.
  - *Moreover* moves us on to a further level of argument, built on what has gone before.
- The use of **hypothesis** (*When she escaped... all Scotland must have sighed; Could any true Englishman want... ?*)

### Persuasive devices

Persuasive language does not usually rely just on argument to make the case: it uses language to drag the reader along. Often this involves **disguising opinion as fact**.

- The use of value-laden **adjectives** (*dear queen, beloved monarch, foolish Queen, turbulent reign, power-crazed King of Spain*).
- Use of **emotive words**, highly charged with emotional meaning (*threat, betrayal, suffered, puppet*).
- **Exaggerated language** (the case against Mary has been not just *proved*, but *proved beyond any shadow of doubt*; Mary didn't just *plot* but *has taken every possible opportunity to plot*).
- Use of constructions which **dare you to disagree**! (*Surely the time has come... Everyone knows that...*) When the author asks, *Could any true Englishman want to exchange...* there is an assumption that anyone who disagrees is not a 'true Englishman'.
- The use of **concession** (*It is clearly difficult for... but... It is hard for... but...*) to counter possible objections.
- **Rhetorical questions** (*Surely the time has come... ? Could any... ?*).
- **Repetition** for effect (*Could any... ? Could anyone... ? for herself, for justice, and for the future of England*).

## Persuasion writing: stage 1

### Content and organisation

- Read examples of persuasive writing and use the 'pronged bullets' skeleton to reduce them to note form: write the points on the left of the bullet and any elaboration on the right (see illustration on text analysis, page 80).

- Choose a controversial issue with which students are familiar and establish a point of view. Ask them to list points on a pronged bullet skeleton. As you compile them, draw attention to the various types of elaboration – explanation, evidence, examples.

### Language features

- Style and vocabulary: study examples of persuasive writing and help students identify elements of persuasive style, such as:
  - value-laden and emotive language, chosen to influence the reader;
  - exaggeration and repetition used for effect;
  - formal vocabulary and constructions, used to give an air of authority.

- Use of connectives to structure an argument. Collect examples from reading, e.g. *if ... then ...; on the other hand; furthermore; moreover; therefore; finally.*

- In Shared Writing, compose a persuasive letter from a fictional character (e.g. Cinderella writing to her sisters to say why she should go to the ball; the Sheriff of Nottingham writing to Robin Hood to evict him from the forest), using as many of the connectives as possible (and demonstrating other aspects of persuasive style, as above). Ask students, in pairs, to write the response, persuasively arguing the case against (e.g. from Robin or the sisters).

### No one forgets a good teacher!

Look at a selection of advertisements past and present.
Help pupils analyse these on a 'pronged bullet' skeleton, e.g.:

Look at this ad!   ✳——— elaboration here is often in terms of
                            visual image, colour, logo, lettering,
Want this product!  ✳——— language-play like alliteration, all of
                            which can appeal to the audience's
Buy it!   ✳——— vanity, conscience, or sense of humour

Discuss the many ways advertisers manipulate their audience. Ask student in pairs to use the skeleton to plan their own advertising campaign (for a school event or and imaginary product) – consisting of a poster and a radio ad with jingle.

## Persuasion writing: stage 2

### Content and organisation

- Read a collection of 'letters to the editor' on current local and national issues. Revise the use of the 'pronged bullets' skeleton to make notes on the main points in these letters, and how each point is elaborated. Evaluate how well the writers have made their points and backed them up. Make a skeleton plan for a letter to the editor on an issue of interest to the students.
- Read our persuasion example (page 79) and plan a similar editorial on a controversial issue in any historical period with which the students are familiar. Make a skeleton plan which can be used later as the basis of writing.

### Language feature

- Persuasive devices: study the use of persuasive devices in our exemplar text (page 80), and list the devices, with short extracts to illustrate them. Ask students to use the constructions to compose single sentences of their own, related to a frivolous topic, e.g.:

*Our dear queen...*
*beloved monarch*
→ *Our beloved*
*Scotch terrier...*
*much-loved pet*

*has taken every*
*possible opportunity*
*to plot*
→ *has taken every*
*possible opportunity*
*to let us know that*
*he is bored.*
*Surely the time has*
*come to take him*
*for a walk...*
*Could any true*
*animal-lover deny*
*him an outing?*
*Could anyone keep*
*this dog penned up*
*for a moment*
*longer...*

## Presenting persuasion

- Organise a balloon debate. Each students chooses a character, alive or dead, whose case s/he would like to argue. Students research their characters, and make skeleton notes (minimum three points, each with elaboration) on why their life should be spared.
- Students should then write a speech, using a range of persuasive devices (as above), pleading their character's case.
- In groups of three, and in the role of their character, students enter the balloon. While flying high above the earth, the balloon's hot air system fails, and two people must be sacrificed so that one can be saved.
- Each character gives a speech arguing his/her claim to live. (Most students will speak better if they work from their skeleton notes. The experience of writing of the speech should improve use of language, especially if they stay in role.)
- On the basis of the speech, the rest of the class each writes down the name of **one** person who must be sacrificed (secret ballot to avoid embarrassment) and the survivor announced.
- If it goes well, you can have play-offs between the various survivors.

## Persuasion writing: stage 3

### *Content and organisation*

- Read a range of persuasion and discussion texts and identify the arguments for and against particular positions. Help students make skeleton notes of these arguments on a for-and-against grid. Note only the main points, not the elaboration.
- Discuss a controversial issue, e.g. post-14 education, homework, the three or four term school year. Create a grid skeleton for points on either side.
- Ask students to choose one side or the other, and turn it into a skeleton for a piece of persuasive writing – i.e. add elaboration to each point (including, where relevant, pre-empting or answering potential objections).

### *Language features*

#### Disguising opinion as fact

- Weasel words. Collect a variety of weasel words writers use for making generalised points, e.g. 'this may/might/could be . . .', 'possibly', 'probably', 'almost always', 'arguably'. Ask students in pairs to choose an opinion (one they're legally/ethically allowed to voice) and lace it with weasel words to turn it into acceptable fact. With the group decide whether each pair of weasel words does the job adequately.
- Look at the examples of 'dare you to disagree', concession and rhetorical questioning in our example (see Persuasive devices, page 81) and ask students to choose one or more of these devices to embellish their opinion. Give each pair the opportunity to declaim their resultant short speech and hold a vote for the most persuasive.

---

### Persuasive writing checklist

#### Organisation

- Does the introductory paragraph contain a clear statement of the case to be argued? ☐
- Does it also contain any background information required by the reader to understand the issue? ☐
- Is each argument clearly stated, preferably with a paragraph to itself? ☐
- Is each argument backed up by any information necessary for the reader to understand? ☐
- Is each argument supported by some form of evidence or examples? ☐
- Does the piece end with a re-statement of the case and a summary of the main points? ☐

#### Language features

- Is the text consistently in the present tense (apart from historical references)? ☐
- Does it contain logical language constructions and connectives? ☐
- Does it contain an appropriate range of persuasive devices to affect the reader, such as:
  - powerful adjectives and other emotive words? ☐
  - constructions such as *Surely . . . It is clear that . . . Everyone knows that . . . ?* ☐
  - the use of questions to make a point? ☐
  - repetition for effect? ☐
- Does the text take opportunities, where appropriate, to answer any likely arguments on the opposite side? ☐

# 3.6 Discussion text

**Purpose**: to present arguments and information from **different viewpoints**.
**Example**: an answer to an essay question.

### Text structure

- Opens with clear statement of **issue** under discussion.
- One of two main types of organisation:
  (a) Arguments **for** + supporting evidence; arguments **against** + supporting evidence, or
  (b) Argument/counter argument, presented one point at a time.
- arguments supported by **evidence and/or examples**;
- reader must be clear which side argues which point;
- skeleton framework – a **for and against** chart.

### Language features

- generally present tense, third person;
- formal, impersonal style;
- logical language constructions and connectives;
- connectives/language constructions to show shifts from one point of view to the other.

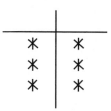

## Key teaching points

- The ability to write discussion text builds on students' persuasive writing. When they can argue one side of a case, they are ready to put both. Discussion, however, generally uses less subjective, value-laden and emotive language than persuasion.
- In everyday life, writers are more often concerned to convey their own point of view than to give a balanced appraisal. Some apparent discussion texts often turn out to be persuasion in disguise (as, possibly, in our example opposite).
- The most likely place to meet discussion is in exams, assessing students' ability to produce reasoned argument. Much discussion, therefore, is 'set piece' writing (see notes on page 89).
- In a short discussion text (as in our example, which had to fit on one side of A4), make all the points for one side then all the points for the other. In a longer discussion, argument and counter-argument may be interwoven, but paragraphing and connectives like *On the other hand...* must ensure the two viewpoints are clearly delineated.

---

Common examples of **discussion text**:

- newspaper editorial;
- non-fiction book on an 'issue';
- exam answer in secondary or tertiary education;
- write-up of a debate;
- formal essay;
- leaflet or article purporting to give balanced account of an issue.

# Do we still need zoos?

Zoos were originally set up so that people could see and learn about wild animals from distant lands. As more people became city-dwellers, never seeing animals in the wild, zoos began to house local creatures too. However, in today's world, are zoos really necessary?

Since people can now see any sort of wild animal in its natural habitat, simply by tuning in to a TV programme or DVD, some animal rights activists claim that zoos are out of date. They argue that it is cruel to capture animals, transport them long distances, and then keep them caged up, simply for the entertainment of human beings. Captive animals often develop 'zoochosis' – abnormal behaviour like rocking or swaying – which indicates that they are bored and unhappy in their prison-like conditions.

On the other hand, there is a huge difference between watching an animal on screen and seeing it in real life. It could be argued that visiting a zoo is educational, often increasing people's concern for wildlife and conservation, which is of great importance in today's developing – and often overdeveloped – world. Indeed, sometimes the only way to save an endangered species may be to arrange for it to breed in captivity. Behind the scenes, zoos also provide scientists with opportunities to research into animal behaviour: modern zoos can therefore be much better planned than old-fashioned ones, providing animals with carefully-designed enclosures appropriate to their needs.

It seems, then, that there are still arguments for retaining zoos. These should, however, be carefully planned with the animals' welfare in mind: in the modern world, there is no excuse for keeping animals in cramped or cruel conditions.

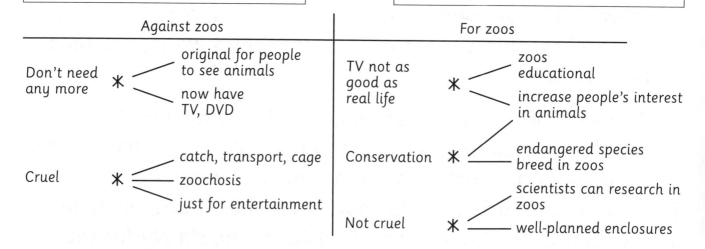

**Purpose**

1 To set out the main arguments on both sides of the case.

2 To come to a reasoned conclusion, based on the facts.

**Audience**

Readers who are interested in the topic and want to know the facts on either side. (Or, possibly, a teacher or examiner who wants to know how well the writer understands the issue.)

| Against zoos | | For zoos | |
|---|---|---|---|
| Don't need any more | ∗ — original for people to see animals / now have TV, DVD | TV not as good as real life | ∗ — zoos educational / increase people's interest in animals |
| Cruel | ∗ — catch, transport, cage / zoochosis / just for entertainment | Conservation | ∗ — endangered species breed in zoos / scientists can research in zoos |
| | | Not cruel | ∗ — well-planned enclosures |

## Organisation and content

**Title:** a question summing up the issue under debate.

### Introduction

Defining the terms of discussion. Three key words in title – *still, need* and *zoos* – suggest that zoos were once necessary, but things may have changed. The introductory paragraph draws attention to these words, clarifying the reason zoos were set up, and reiterating the question.

### Argument

**Paragraph 2:** The argument against zoos.
First sentence states why zoos are no longer needed to perform the function defined in the introduction (argument 1).
Second sentence gives a reason for disbanding them (argument 2).
Third sentence elaborates this point (scientific evidence).

**Paragraph 3:** The argument in favour of zoos.
First sentence contests argument 1.
Second sentence elaborates, converting the argument into an up-to-date reason for maintaining zoos.
Third sentence elaborates this new argument (further detail).
Fourth and fifth sentences contest argument 2 (point + elaboration).

### Conclusion

**Final paragraph:**
First sentence provides an answer to the question posed in the title, based on argument 1.
Second sentence sums up the implications of argument 2.

---

#### Do we still need zoos?

Zoos were originally set up so that people could see and learn about wild animals from distant lands. As more people became city-dwellers, never seeing animals in the wild, zoos began to house local creatures too. However, in today's world, are zoos really necessary?

Since people can now see any sort of wild animal in its natural habitat, simply by tuning in to a TV programme or DVD, some animal rights activists claim that zoos are out of date. They argue that it is cruel to capture animals, transport them long distances, and then keep them caged up, simply for the entertainment of human beings. Captive animals often develop 'zoochosis' – abnormal behaviour like rocking or swaying – which indicates that they are bored and unhappy in their prison-like conditions.

On the other hand, there is a huge difference between watching an animal on screen and seeing it in real life. It could be argued that visiting a zoo is educational, often increasing people's concern for wildlife and conservation, which is of great importance in today's developing – and often overdeveloped – world. Indeed, sometimes the only way to save an endangered species may be to arrange for it to breed in captivity. Behind the scenes, zoos also provide scientists with opportunities to research into animal behaviour: modern zoos can therefore be much better planned than old-fashioned ones, providing animals with carefully-designed enclosures appropriate to their needs.

It seems, then, that there are still arguments for retaining zoos. These should, however, be carefully planned with the animals' welfare in mind: in the modern world, there is no excuse for keeping animals in cramped or cruel conditions.

---

### Form and style

- Discussion text – general, impersonal, formal.
- Terms of discussion must be clearly defined.

- Two sides of an argument clearly set out.
- Layout must reflect the argument – paragraphs.

---

## Language features

### General language

- Apart from historical references, written in the **present tense**, because the issue is a current one.
- References to *people, activists, scientists, animals, wildlife* etc. (generalised participants), because this is a general argument, not just about one particular zoo.

### Formal impersonal language

Discussions call for formal written language patterns, indicating that the arguments have been carefully considered and composed. They also require an impersonal stance: the personal opinions of the writer are unimportant.

- Written in the **third person** using generalised 'voices' for the two sides of the debate (*activists – they*).
- Occasional use of the **passive voice** (e.g. *It could be argued*) which is formal and impersonal, and avoids the question of who exactly is arguing the point.
- Frequent use of **formal vocabulary** (e.g. *originally* rather than *first;* habitat rather than *home; indicates* rather than *shows*). On the whole, formal vocabulary has its roots in the classical languages and is associated with written language and formal situations. The simpler words we associate with speech and directness tend to have Old English origins.
- Frequent use of **complex sentences** (see The language of ideas, below) which are a feature of formal written language.

### The language of ideas

- Discussions are often about abstract ideas, so many of the terms used are **abstract nouns** (things you cannot see or touch), e.g. *entertain-*

*ment, zoochosis, concern, conservation, importance, difference, captivity, research, welfare.*

- **Complex sentences** often show the logical relationships between the ideas expressed in clauses, e.g. in the first two paragraphs the **conjunctions** *so that... As...* and *Since...* all show cause and effect.
- **Connectives** between sentences also show logical relationships:
  - *However... On the other hand...* both indicate that an alternative viewpoint is about to be expressed;
  - *Indeed...* suggests an accumulation of facts;
  - *... therefore* indicates cause and effect;
  - *... then...* at the beginning of the final paragraph suggests that we have arrived at a logical conclusion.
- **Punctuation** can also be used to indicate links between ideas: the **semicolon** in the final sentence of paragraph 3 and the **colon** in the final sentence both suggest a causal links.
- the use of the **conditional form** of the verb (*It could be argued... may be to...*) indicates that the writer is dealing in hypothesis. It also distances the author from the argument.

### Expressing both sides of the debate

- **Paragraph breaks** are used to help show the division between the two points of view.
- Generalised terms are used to indicate **general participants** on one side of the debate, e.g. *some animal rights activists claim...*
- The **passive voice** (*it could be argued...*) is used in the same way to indicate the opposing view.
- **Connectives** like *however...* and *On the other hand...* show that an opposing view is about to be voiced.

## Discussion writing

### *Content and organisation*

- Read examples of discussion text and help students convert them into skeleton notes, i.e. a for-and-against grid, with pronged bullets (point + elaboration) on each side.
- Investigate the organisation of the text and in each case establish which type of construction the author has chosen:
  1 Arguments for + supporting evidence/ Arguments against + supporting evidence.
  2 Argument/counter-argument presented one point at a time.
- Create skeleton notes for a discussion piece on a topic familiar to students.

### *Language features*

- Language conventions of discursive texts; formal impersonal language. Use the exemplar texts to discuss general features of discussion language (see text analysis and checklist).
- Complex sentences; formal impersonal language. Take some complex sentences from an exemplar text, e.g. *Since people can now see any sort of wild animal in its natural habitat…some animal rights activists claim that zoos are out of date…*and turn them into a mini-speaking frame (see page 11): *Since _____, some _____ activists claim that _____.* Demonstrate, and then ask students in pairs to make up sentences on other topics that fit into the frame, e.g. **Since** *aeroplanes are responsible for high levels of dangerous emissions,* **some** *environmental* **activists claim** *that there should be much higher taxation on air travel.* By manipulating and speaking these language patterns themselves, students become familiar with complex sentence constructions and the language of argument.

## Conditional language

*If all the world **were** paper, and all the sea **were** ink,*
*And all the trees were bread and cheese, what **would** we have to drink?*

Make a collection of conditional constructions used in discussion texts, e.g. *It **could** be claimed that…This **might** mean that…It is **possible** that…This would **perhaps** result in…* Establish that much argument is hypothetical; authors should use conditional constructions when making statements for which they have no evidence.

Conditional language involves some changes to the verb form (notably *will* ➔ *would*, but also, if you're being pernickety, *was* ➔ *were*, as in the traditional rhyme above).

Ask students to use sentence starts like the ones above to create spoken sentences about familiar subjects. There are many more oral activities of this kind in *Speaking Frames: How to Teach Talk for Writing: Ages 10–14.*

## Discussion checklist

### Organisation

- Does the introductory paragraph clearly state the issue under discussion picking up any key words from the title? ☐
- Are the arguments on each side of the debate clearly stated? ☐
- Is each argument supported by evidence, explanation or examples? ☐
- Do the paragraph breaks help the reader clearly see both sides of the argument? ☐
- Is there a final paragraph in which a conclusion is reached, based on the arguments? ☐

### Language features

- Is the text consistently in the present tense (apart from historical references)? ☐
- Are the arguments presented in the third person, using:
    - generalised voices (e.g. *Some people claim...*)? ☐
    - the passive voice (e.g. *It is argued that...*)? ☐
- Does the text use formal impersonal language and formal vocabulary? ☐
- Are links made clear by the use of logical connectives (e.g. *Therefore, Consequently*) and connectives showing the onset of an alternative viewpoint (e.g. *On the other hand..., However...*)? ☐
- Is there use of conditional language (*It may be... It could be...*) to suggest possibility or hypothesis? ☐

## Formal essays

The most common form of discussion writing is the formal essay, and these don't crop up very often in everyday life – they tend to be something you do as part of school-work or examinations. The **audience** for formal essays, therefore, is usually a teacher or an exam marker, and the **purpose** is to impress them that you know:

(a)  all the facts about the subject;
(b)  how to structure a formal essay.

This is not a very natural writing situation! The checklist below can help you make a good job of it.

### When writing a formal essay or exam question

- carefully state the issue under discussion, attending to the terms of reference (i.e. what are the key words in the title?);
- don't lose track of these key words – keep them at the heart of your discussion;
- make points clearly and provide plenty of elaboration (explanatory detail, supporting evidence, examples) – don't wander off the point;
- keep 'for' and 'against' arguments clearly separated;
- return to the issue at the end, summarising the main points and, if required, offering an answer to the question, based on the arguments;
- remember that the person marking the essay is not interested in your personal opinion, but in how well you know the facts and are able to argue the case;
- however, if you do have an opinion, use your interest in the subject to help you press the case well.

# Appendix: Supporting writing across the curriculum in secondary schools

Effective teaching of writing across the curriculum involves commitment by teachers throughout the school, many of whom are not English specialists. The 'two horses' teaching model suggested in this book allows English teachers to use students' cross-curricular knowledge as the basis for teaching specific literacy skills. This should be advantageous for all teachers:

- non-English specialists are relieved of responsibility for *teaching* writing skills, allowing them to concentrate on their own subject area;
- English specialists have ready-made meaningful content for literacy lessons, which they can use to develop students' speaking and writing skills.

Since effort is no longer being duplicated (possibly at cross-purposes) it should also free up time for all teachers to provide more opportunities for 'active learning', especially for developing ideas and understanding through talk.

It will probably fall to English teachers to explain the system to colleagues. The information required by non-English specialists is covered in:

- Part 1, pages 1–8 ('Two horses' and 'Talk for learning');
- the three photocopiable handouts provided in this Appendix.

However, it's never a good idea to go blind into these things. Before attempting to bring all colleagues on board, it helps to have a trial run of the system with a couple of non-English specialists from different disciplines. As well as identifying potential problems (and, hopefully, their solutions), trialing provides in-house expertise from a range of subject fields.

The point of the two horse model and the skeletons is that they are *very* simple and *very* basic. My experience is that the simpler the system, the more useful it is in allowing teachers to realise their own professional talents.

The point of all systems should be to support human relationships, and successful cross-curricular work depends on successful relationships between teachers throughout a school. The idea of this book is to support those relationships. However, whenever you find that teachers are working pointlessly to supporting a creaking system – whether the one I recommend or any other – please get together and overthrow it.

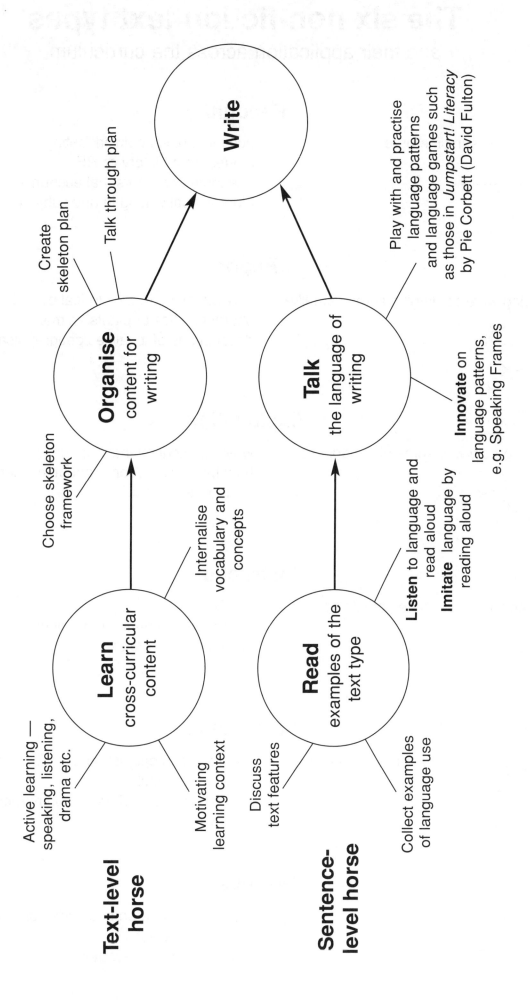

**Write**

Talk through plan

Create skeleton plan

**Organise** content for writing

Choose skeleton framework

Internalise vocabulary and concepts

**Learn** cross-curricular content

Active learning — speaking, listening, drama etc.

Motivating learning context

Discuss text features

**Text-level horse**

Play with and practise language patterns and language games such as those in *Jumpstart! Literacy* by Pie Corbett (David Fulton)

**Talk** the language of writing

**Innovate** on language patterns, e.g. Speaking Frames

**Listen** to language and read aloud

**Imitate** language by reading aloud

**Read** examples of the text type

Collect examples of language use

**Sentence-level horse**

© 2011 Sue Palmer, *How to Teach Writing Across the Curriculum: Ages 8–14*. London: Routledge.

# The six non-fiction text types
## and their application across the curriculum

## Recount

retelling events in time order

accounts of schoolwork/outings
stories from history or RE
anecdotes and personal accounts
biographical writing in any subject

## Report

describing what something is (or was) like

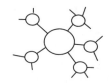

aspects of life in a historical period
characteristics of plants/animals
descriptions of localities/geographical features

## Explanation

explaining how/why something happens

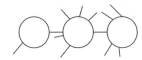

why historical events happened
how things work/come about in science,
geography, etc.

## Instruction

telling how to do or make something

art, DT, PE activities
procedures in maths/ICT/science
class or school rules

## Persuasion

arguing a case; trying to influence opinion

'publicity campaigns' (articles, posters, leaflets)
in any subject
expressing viewpoints on controversial topics in
any subject

## Discussion

a balanced argument

stating the case on both sides of a controversy
in any subject
writing objective 'essays'

# The key ingredients of non-fiction text types

| Recount | Report | Explanation | Instruction | Persuasion | Discussion |
|---|---|---|---|---|---|
| **Audience** Someone who is interested in what happened | **Audience** Someone who wants to know about something | **Audience** Someone who wants to understand a process | **Audience** Someone who wants to know how to do something | **Audience** Someone you are trying to influence | **Audience** Someone who is interested in an issue |
| **Purpose** To tell the reader what happened in an informative and entertaining way | **Purpose** To present information so that it is easy to find and understand | **Purpose** To help someone understand a process | **Purpose** To tell someone how to do something clearly | **Purpose** To promote a particular view in order to influence what people do or think | **Purpose** To help someone understand the issue |
| **Examples** <br>• autobiography <br>• newspaper article <br>• history book | **Examples** <br>• dictionary <br>• reference book <br>• text books | **Examples** <br>• car manual <br>• encyclopaedia <br>• science text book | **Examples** <br>• recipe <br>• instruction manual | **Examples** <br>• adverts <br>• fliers <br>• newspaper editorial | **Examples** <br>• news feature <br>• essay on causes of something e.g. global warming |
| **Typical structure** <br>• paragraphs organised in chronological order | **Typical structure** <br>• paragraphs – not in chronological order <br>• often organised in categories with headings/sub-headings | **Typical structure** <br>• series of logical steps explaining how or why something occurs | **Typical structure** <br>• chronological order <br>• often in list form <br>• diagrams, visual | **Typical structure** <br>• often a series of points supporting one viewpoint <br>• logical order | **Typical structure** <br>• paragraphs <br>• often a series of contrasting points <br>• logical order |
| **Typical language features** <br>• past tense <br>• first or third person <br>• time connectives | **Typical language features** <br>• formal and impersonal <br>• technical vocabulary <br>• present tense <br>• generalises <br>• detail where necessary | **Typical language features** <br>• casual connectives <br>• technical vocabulary <br>• formal and impersonal <br>• present tense | **Typical language features** <br>• simple and clear formal English <br>• imperative <br>• numbers or time connectives | **Typical language features** <br>• emotive language <br>• personal language <br>• weasel phrases | **Typical language features** <br>• present tense <br>• formal and impersonal <br>• logical connectives |

With thanks to Julia Strong of the National Literacy Trust